"A Concise Primer on Starting Your New Business!

Visit us at
StartupGuideTo.com

Startup Guide
TO
Be Your Own BOSS

FOLLOW YOUR PASSION

BUSINESS PLAN

CEO

Brian Cochran, D.M.

A Reference For The Beginner

Startup Guide to Be Your Own Boss

By Dr. Brian Cochran

Published by Biz Help 101

Biz Help 101 books, guides, and manuals may be ordered by contacting:

Biz Help 101
1107 E. Grand Ave. #A,
Pomona, Ca. 91766
www.BizHelp101.com
1-647-204-6249

Printed in the United States of America
Biz Help 101 date: 4/25/2013

Table of Contents

My Dad Nudged Me Into It!

I have been a serial entrepreneur most of my life. My first business came about because my parents give us a weekly allowance and it was not enough for some of the things that I wanted. We weren't poor, we were considered upper middle class. My dad did me a favor I didn't understand it at the time but when I would ask for a raise on my allowance he would say go get a job, I was about 11 or 12 at the time. I learned how to mow & edge our lawn. I wanted a new pair of Converse sneakers they just came out with the color red and I already had a pair of white, but I wanted to have a red pair as well. So I asked my day if I could use the lawn mower and edger to go and make some extra money. He said yes with a condition, return it in the same condition it left in including gas.
What a powerful lessons my dad gave me to take charge of my life to be able to generate my own income, even at the age of 12. I learned that I didn't have to depend on any one but myself to make a living.
So off I went and started my own lawn care service. I will never forget what independence I had, and wonderful it felt when I finished the job for a client and they paid me. I was able to build 12 accounts and made enough money that I didn't need or desire an allowance from my parents. I maintained his tools, kept it full of gas and made pretty good money for a 12 year old.

As I got older, about 14 I became interested in becoming a party planner. My house was the party house coming up. My parents lived for the weekend, on Friday my dad would go to the store and stock up with liquor, chips, cold cuts, everything needed to have a party. Did I say almost every weekend? There would be at least 10 to 15 people every weekend at our house watching sports and having a house party.

My parents gave me another life lesson on hospitality and benefits. My dad used to say "do it at home" meaning instead of getting in trouble in the streets do it at home. So I put him to the test! I organized a party at my house, and 300+ showed up. There was so many people that the police closed off the street and the only people that could get on our street was the people that lived in the neighborhood. That started my career as an event planner, which I still operate that business. The success of that and many other events caused an organization that was event planners to mentor me into my destiny.

Following Your Passion

I can remember how on weekends before we went anywhere or did anything we had to clean the house. At that time 45's and LP's records were the thing, so we would go to the record store and purchase all the latest music at that time. So we have a large collection of music. I know all the latest music at that time and we would play records as we cleaned and it was a family day and project.

From knowing the music (product knowledge) and living it I became passionate about the music industry. It was a perfect match because of being an event planner I had knowledge of trends and planned events around the music industry.

One day at one of our events the DJ (Disc Jockey) didn't show up and there was approximately 1000 people at the event. I borrowed my home stereo and records and DJ the event. By the way, I wasn't that good but I had the passion. We got through the event and that became another phase of my entrepreneurship life. My passion drove me to learn all I could about being a DJ, at that time I was about 15 almost 16 years old. So I went to every record store in southern California, looked up every DJ I could find so I could learn the art and business of being a DJ. My passion drove me to being a DJ on several popular radio stations, I ended up getting hired and working at some of the largest clubs in the world at that time. All because of following my passion and going for it. I didn't let my age, color, or any limitation store from reaching my goal and passion. Passion will fuel you to walk through fire to get to your destiny. At 16, I was very successful and had tow divisions of my business. I was an event planner and a DJ.

Success Draws

I'm not bragging, but I became a local success and people sought me out to ask me how did I do what I do. I was young and didn't understand about being a professional and an authority in marketing, and event planning.

Where you build your business become the authority in that field so that people will seek you instead of you going after them.

Customers want to do business with successful in the know people in the field of what they want or need. At the time I didn't seek after people to use my services as a marketing guy, but from the success in the other fields, people came to me to market and promote their business.

The Go to Guy

I became the guy to go to for business, because of my success and people saw it they wanted to be successful and they attached themselves to me. I had multiple streams of income and didn't even know what that meant. I just saw it as an opportunity to keep myself ahead of my competition and most of all following my passion.

Because of my notoriety, and what appeared to be success my client base was not just in the music-party industry, it extended to being a marketing consultant for restaurants, realtors, hair salons and so on…

You want to be the go to guy or girl, this means that you must become the expert in your field, so that people will chase you. It has to become a part of your plan and DNA.

I can go on, but I think you get it!

What's on your house

As you have just read my businesses and being an entrepreneur started from what was in my house. Millionaires have been built from finding the opportunity(ies) found in their own home.

One of my favorite shows is called "Shark Tank" and on the show is a man named Daymond John. He and some friends started a company from his home and from the trunk of his car called FUBU. That company that founded in the home became a $500,000,000 a year company at its peak. His passion to be in the clothing industry drove him into his destiny. Now he is on a hit national TV show, is sought business consultant know as a branding specialist.

There is a story in the bible about this woman who had lost her husband and her 2 boys were going to be sold into slavery to pay off the debt that the family had. So she went to a Prophet of God and he asked her a question "What's In Your House!" She had a couple of small empty pots and one that had oil in it. The man of god told her to go to her neighbors and borrow some vessels and come back to him. So she did what was asked and he prayed and filled all the vessels with oil. He told her to go and sell the oil and pay off the debt. So the woman and her sons did what was asked and was able to pay off the debt. There was much left over and the prophet told her to use that remaining to us to make money.

So, I'm asking you want is in your house? There is a large company called EBay and that company had empowered millions of people to become entrepreneurs. Taking what was in their house and sold it through EBay and have made a living and even millionaires were made as will starting with what was in their homes.

The opportunities are there, you just have to be open to it and look. Most people don't go into business because they are not open and fearful. Because your reading his book you're already ahead of the game. By educating yourself empowers and prepares you towards success.

Characteristics of a Successful Entrepreneur

There are several characteristics of being a successful entrepreneur and

- *Guts:* Guts mean you must have an entrepreneurial instinct, which is an overwhelming desire to have your own business. You must have the guts and dedication to be completely devoted to your goal. Incidentally, devotion to your goal is much more likely if you have a love for your intended business. Life is too short to start a business that doesn't give you satisfaction and joy. And, through good times and bad times, you will stick with something you love. As Solomon said, "There is nothing better for men (and women!) than they should be happy in their work-so let them enjoy it now."

- *Brains:* While appropriate educational credentials are important, entrepreneurial "brains" means more than scholastic achievements. To become a successful entrepreneur, you should have a working knowledge about the business you plan to start **before you start it**. Common sense, combined with appropriate experience, is the necessary brainpower. Prudence, follow through and attention to detail are very important.

- *Capital:* Every business needs money of your own plus sufficient cash to maintain a positive cash flow for at least a year. In a future session operating entrepreneurs will learn how to forecast future cash requirements through cash flow control. Many businesses can be started on a very small scale with a small investment. Then, as the business grows and you gain experience, cash flow from your business can be used for growth. In some cases, you don't need starting capital to hire other people because you might start by doing everything yourself. The "do it yourself" start is a good way to learn everything about your business and also makes you better qualified to delegate work to others later on. You can control your risk by placing a limit on how much you invest in your business.

- **Perseverance**: You must have thick skin, because success that happen overnight. A lot of entrepreneurs give up too soon and not push through the difficult times in starting in managing and growing your business. Successful people turn obstacles into opportunities, By looking at a problem and knowing that there is a solution and pressing towards the goal of building a successful business.

- **Passionate**: You will do whatever it takes in order to make a success. Passion is the fuel to drive you in building your business, even when your business is at a loss, you won't give up. Successful entrepreneurs are passionate about the field that they are in and it shows with the enthusiasm and excitement that you show in their business.

Step 1: Create a Life Plan

Plan your life, then plan your business.

As I always say, plan your life, *then* plan your business.

Some of the most successful and happy people we know are entrepreneurs who created a business that's in perfect synchronicity with what they want out of life. If you do what you love, you'll work harder, better and more happily. Planning your life fuels you to drive towards your goals in building a business that will give you the resources to do what it is where you would like your life to end up. If you plan to retire, what will that look like? How much will it cost to live at your retirement age? If you would like to leave an inheritance for you children, how much would you like to leave them?

In this step we will focus on:

- Elements of your Life Plan
- Using your Life Plan

Elements of your Life Plan:

Your Current Status

Think carefully and honestly about where you are now in your life. Consider work, recreation, relationships, finances and anything else that's important to you. And then jot down some simple, succinct bullet points in each of these categories:

- Quality rating of your life on a scale of 1 through 100, with 100 being the best possible life
- Realities of your life, including responsibilities, funds available to start a business, expenses
- Things that make you happy
- Things that make you unhappy

Your Ideal Life

This is a snapshot of your "ideal" life, in a very brief, bulleted list. And remember, the sky's the limit, so don't be afraid of being bold or maybe even a little grandiose. Factor in things like family time, hobbies, charity work, early retirement – anything that gets you *really* excited.

Your Loves: What You Really Like Doing

Think about the types of things that you love to do, whether at work, at home, or at your local soup kitchen. List these things out briefly. And don't worry if some themes are starting to repeat in each section, that just means you have some really focused ideas about what you want in life!

Your Skills & Capabilities: What You Do Well

List the abilities, experience and strengths you can build on to attain that ideal life. Bear in mind that your skills need not be strictly from your professional life – list skills developed in your personal life as well. It may be a combination of skills that leads you to a startup that's best suited to fit your needs.

Your Track Record: What You Have Experience Doing

List those accomplishments in your professional and personal life of which you're most proud. Pay particular attention to successes you've had that would be helpful in starting a business and managing it successfully. Having experience in a certain area will help in the learning curve in starting a business.

Your Ideal Work Style

Whether full-time or part-time, at-home or on the road, working behind the scenes or interacting with lots of people — understand what your work style priorities are so you can define the best kind of business for you.

Another way to look at this is, what level of risk do you want to take? You may want a relatively low-pressure first-go at entrepreneurship.

You may have to stay on your job until _____. (You fill in the blank) .

Your Manifesto

This is your personal mission, your values and what drives you forward, all wrapped up into a one-page (maximum) statement. To write this, you should draw on everything you've already discovered about yourself in steps 1 through 6, and bring it all together into a clear statement of your principles and priorities.

Our example manifesto

Work as Freedom: We think work is about pursuing our dreams, not for the benefit of some nameless, faceless company, but for ourselves. We believe that owning our own business leads to the liberties and freedoms that the forefathers of our country envisioned for us. We're free to choose the kind of business we conduct. We're free to choose the way we spend our time. We're free to choose the people with whom we work. We're free to set our priorities.

Work as Family: We've tried to create a workplace environment where employees feel like they're actually members of a greater family. There's a sense of common purpose, mutual respect, and deep trust. Everyone should feel important and as though they're a meaningful member of the collective effort. It's an environment that empowers people to share in the hard work—and in the benefits.

Work as Fulfillment: We've made it a priority to ensure that our work gives us a sense of satisfaction. When we wake up in the morning, we can't wait to get on the phone, get online, and get our team in gear. The work we do is truly the work we love. For us there's nothing that turns us on more than facing a challenge and transforming it into an opportunity. There's nothing more thrilling than seeing a customer use our product. There's nothing more gratifying than helping someone else turn a dream into a real business. And over time, we've found that our fulfillment comes as much from the process of trying to achieve our goals as it does from actually achieving them.

Key Moves to Get You Where You Want to Go

These are simple strategic action items you must develop in order to transform your Life Plan from a self-assessment into an action plan. At this point in life planning, you know where you want to go, what skills you already have, as well as what type of work suits you best. Draw from that information a list of moves you'll need to make to achieve your ideal life.

Take your time in this area and search your soul and write it out. Knowing where you want to go again will be the driving force to getting there.

I always ask my student the following statement: I live just outside of Los Angeles, Ca. "Can you get to New York City by only taking the Interstate 10 Freeway? The answer is NO! You must chart out a course to get to New York, which is the same way to planning your life. If your goal is to be wealthy, what is wealthy to you? Is it a million dollars or 1 billion dollars? Knowing how much money you need to make a day, month, year will help you to become what you want financially.

Using your Life Plan

It's very important to print your Life Plan and keep it in plain view. You'll find that its presence—even in your peripheral vision—will constantly remind you of what you want, what's important, and what to do next.

The difference between a vision and a dream? A vision has been acted on by writing it down and a dream is in your head.

Ideally, you should also revisit your Life Plan periodically to measure your success and to make adjustments and additions where appropriate. It's okay if things change over time—life is a fluid and dynamic thing and your Life Plan should be, too!

Use your Life Plan to provide context for strategic decisions you make—including what niche you choose to operate in, what business model you'll use, whether you'll have lots of employees or a home-based, one person operation.

Most importantly, your Life Plan will position you to do what you LOVE and that always brings out the best in an entrepreneur…

Step-by-Step Approach (Pre- Startup)

Decide if you really want to be in business:

You are putting some (not all, hopefully) of your net worth at risk. You may run the risk of becoming eccentric, meaning creating a life that is out of balance, with working hours taking away from other family or pleasurable activities. There may be levels of stress you have not experienced as an employee. So be prepared!

Decide what business and where:

Once you are satisfied you have the characteristics of a successful entrepreneur and that you definitely want to be in business, then you must decide which business is best for you and where to locate that business. If you want a brick and mortar, Internet, or Home-based? They all have their strengths and weaknesses and the good thing about being an entrepreneur is that you can change directions when need be. Selection strategy is covered later on in this session. Also see our home-based and Internet business session for those considering operating a business from their home. I will go into more details in this chapter.

Decide whether to operate full-time or moonlight:

There are some interesting advantages and some pitfalls in operating as a moonlight business. (That is, a business you start in your off hours while still working at your current job.) More often than not, the advantages of starting as a moonlighter outweigh the risks:

- You avoid burning your bridges of earnings including retirement, health and fringe benefits and vacations.
- Your full-time job won't suffer if you maintain certain conflict of interest disciplines, including compartmentalizing your job and business into completely separate worlds.
- You can avoid conflict of interest with your job by choosing a business that is appropriate for moonlighting, such as single products, real estate, specialized food, e-commerce, direct marketing or family-run operations.

There are great advantages for operating a family business. If you are a moonlighter the family can run the business while you are at work. You have a built-in organizational structure. You can teach your kids the benefits of being in business.

But there are also some pitfalls to consider in starting a moonlight business:

- There is a temptation to spend time at your job working on your moonlight business. That is unfair to your employer and should not be done under any circumstances. (You may need a family member or some trusted person to cover emergencies when you are at your job.)
- Another problem may be competing with your employer, which is not right. Think of how you would feel or handle this employee if you were the boss.
- Any kind of conflict with your regular work can jeopardize your job and your moonlight business.
- Overwork and mental and physical exhaustion can also become a very real problem for moonlight entrepreneurs.

A special message for people in transition:
If you happen to be unemployed and are thinking about starting a business, Biz Help 101's "Business Start-up 101 course will offer some suggestions.

Selection Strategy

Operating the wrong business is the most frequent mistake that start-up entrepreneurs make. Here is a checklist to help you to evaluate if you are in a potentially successful one or to reassess the business you are in:
If you have not yet selected a business, take your time and wait for the business that is just right for you. You will not be penalized for missing opportunities. The selection process takes a lot of planning and your experience and complete knowledge is vital for your success.

- A common problem is not having much money to start a business. Surprisingly, there are a number of businesses that require no money at all. Please click on "Show Me the money" from our session 4 on financing a business.

- Don't tackle or pursue businesses that may be too challenging. It is better to identify a one-foot hurdle than try to jump a seven-footer.

- Try to identify a business that has long-term economic potential. Follow Wayne Gretzky's advice, "Go to where the puck is going, not to where it is."

- A big mistake can be an error of omission. This means you may fail to see an opportunity that is right in front of you.

- Keep in mind that as a general rule specialists do better than non-specialists. Wouldn't you be more inclined to take your sick cat to a veterinarian whose practice is limited to cats rather than to a general practitioner?

- Operate a business that will grow in today's and tomorrow's markets. Many small retail stores are no longer in business because huge stores such as Wal-Mart and Home Depot provide more choices to the customer and often at a cheaper price.

- Follow the advice of Chairman Warren Buffett, of Berkshire-Hathaway Inc. and the most successful business picker in American history. Mr. Buffett looks for businesses that focus on a "consumer monopoly" with pricing power and long-term predictable growth prospects. Here are two books that will give you invaluable insights into how Mr. Buffett selects businesses in which to invest. You can copycat these basic principles to help select your own business.

- Businesses to avoid are "commodity" businesses where you must compete entirely on price and in which you must have the lowest cost to survive. As Mr. Buffett has said, "In a commodity type business you're only as smart as your dumbest competitor."

- Most service businesses have pricing power. Pricing power means that you will not need to have the lowest price in order to secure business. Your customers will be willing to pay a fair price for a better product or service.

- Should you bet on a business you don't know when you can bet on a business you do know?

- If you are manufacturing a product, consider the pros and cons of contracting out production to a low-cost supplier. In other words, operate a "hollow corporation." A "hollow corporation" is a company that subcontracts manufacturing and packaging.

- If your business is based on marketing an invention or patent, keep these ideas in mind:
  a. First check to determine if there are any issued patents similar to your idea. You can secure information from the U.S. Patent office at www.uspto.gov.
  b. Be cautious about getting involved with firms that ask for up-front fees to market an invention.
  c. No matter what you hope for, you will need a product to test, to show and to solicit feedback.

Things to Watch Out For

- Impatience
- Do not let over confidence short-circuit you from analyzing your business carefully. You must not fear hearing the negative aspects; it is much better to be aware of them and face them early on.
- The lure of high rewards. They will come if you have selected the right business and if you understand every aspect of the business before you open its doors.

Suggestions For People In Transition

More people than ever are victims, or are about to be victims, of downsizing: also known as "reduction in force", "made redundant", or "your job just went overseas". Scary questions begin to arise: Where do I go from here? How am I going to make my mortgage payment?

For a laid-off worker who doesn't have bright prospects for replacing his or her job, there is a possibility not to be overlooked - Why not go into business for yourself? For those still in jobs but fearful of losing them (the signs are usually evident), there is the possibility of starting a moonlight business now, while still working.

Required Activities

It is worth repeating: The most common mistake — and the most costly one — is not selecting the right business initially. This is the time for soul-searching for operating entrepreneurs.

IF YOU HAVE NOT YET DECIDED ON A BUSINESS, DO THIS:

On the top of a blank sheet of paper, write an activity you like to perform (make this the heading). Do a separate page for each activity or interest you have.

On those same sheets list as many businesses you can think of that are related to that activity.

On the same sheets, list all the products or services you can think of that are related to that activity. Use your imagination and think of every possible product or service you could perform.

Make a list of businesses that do better in bad times (one may be appropriate for you). Some examples might be pawnshops, auto repairs and fabric stores.

If you just want to get your feet wet we have designed a way for people to make money by selling various products and services online. Having your own Internet ecommerce business. I know it's a cheap plug, but it works and we have many people are generating a great income doing so.

There are many other companies that offer what is called "affiliate marketing." Affiliate Marketing is where a person takes what is called banner ads and promotes those business products or services and generates a small commission on a person clicks through to the sales page of the products or service being sold. Using your database you would market to them about what they are offering.

17

POSSIBLE BUSINESS EXAMPLE

Let's assume you end up with three potential businesses: towing service, used car sales and auto repairs. You can now make a comparative evaluation using the following checklist (or better still your own checklist) with a 1-10 scoring system. This kind of analysis can help you gain objectivity in selecting your business.

Objective	Towing Service	Used Car Sales	Auto Repair
Can I do what I love to do?	6	3	10
Will I fill an expanding need?	8	5	10
Can I specialize?	7	8	10
Can I learn it and test it first?	9	8	9

This kind of analysis can help you gain objectivity in selecting your business.

How to Evaluate the Business

Here are some questions to help clarify your thoughts:

- *Is it something I will enjoy doing?* As Harvey McKay has said, "Find something you love to do and you'll never have to work a day in your life." Also, if you're doing something you love, you're much more likely to stick with it through thick and thin times.
  My favorite activities are _____
  I like to serve people by _____
- *Will it serve an expanding need for which there is no close substitute?*
- *Can I be so good at a specialized, targeted need that customers will think there is no close substitute?* For example, in California, nobody comes close to See's Candies.
- *Can I handle the capital requirements?*
- *Can I learn the business by working for someone else first?* Our favorite example: if you're planning to open a convenience store, for heaven's sake go to work for a national chain first!
- One option for going into business is buying a business or a franchise.
- An entire session in our course Building My Own Business is devoted to buying businesses. In many cases, buying a business is less risky than starting from scratch.

- *Could I operate as a hollow corporation, without a factory and with a minimum number of employees?* For example, if you have in mind marketing a line of furniture, you might consider outsourcing to a manufacturing vendor in China. Cost savings is often the prime objective, but you also free up your time and capital. The major risk is the performance of the vendor and your success in developing good relationships that provide mutual benefits.
- *Is this a product or service that I can test first?* Your concept of a successful product or service may not be in harmony with the reality of the market place. On a small scale, prove it out first. As Wolfgang Puck states: "I learned more from the one restaurant that didn't work than from all the ones that were successes."
- *Should I consider a partner who has complementary skills or who could help finance the business?*

Use a "For" and "Against" List to Evaluate your Business

Make a "for" and "against" list regarding characteristics of the business. On a blank piece of paper, draw a vertical line down the middle of the page and list on one side all the "fors" and on the other all the "againsts." Sometimes this will help clarify your thinking. We have provided a "for" and "against" template for you to use.

Write down the names of at least five successful businesses in your chosen field. Analyze what these five businesses have in common and make a list of reasons for their success.

Talk to several people in your intended business. Don't be afraid of the negative aspects of your intended business. Instead, seek out the pitfalls — better now than after you open your doors. Take notes if possible. Write down the information as soon as you can.

Analyze the competition that are not doing well and write down the reasons.

Get Completely Qualified

Before you proceed further in your business, get completely qualified:

- The best way to become qualified is to go to work for someone in the same business.
- Attend all classes you can on the skills you need: for example, accounting, computing and selling.
- Read all the "How To" books you can. Here are three good examples:

Initial Startup Checklist

The following is a step-by-step list of considerations, questions, steps and tasks that should be considered, completed and/or initiated when forming a business.

1. Decide on the type of business and what product or service you will offer.

2. Decide the method of how you are going to market and sell your goods and services.

3. Create a name for the business.

4. Decide what business structure you will use to operate your company.

5. Decide in which state you will form the business structure and the jurisdictions you will do business in.

6. Put your corporate structure in compliance immediately after it's formed.

7. Develop a written Business and Marketing plan for your business start and growth.

8. Create an image and brand for your company.

9. Produce a web site and marketing materials to promote and sell your product and services.

10. Find a mentor or resource for business advice.

Choosing a Business Type

A few important decisions need to be made when choosing a business type.

1. Do you want to buy an existing business, create your own or invest in a franchise?

2. Do you want to sell a product or service?

3. Do you want to sell Business to Consumer or Business to Business?

There tends to be an equal number of benefits to buy an existing business, creating your own and investing in a franchise, that we cannot tell you one is better than another. It's fun to create something of your own from scratch. It's great to see what someone else has done to be successful and what mistakes they have made so you don't make them again. It's also advantageous to purchase an existing brand name and have systems already created by a franchisor. In the end, it's completely up to you in deciding which type of business you should start.

Choosing a product or service is not an either/or. You can decide to sell products as well as services.

Many people who offer a service have become an expert in their field. That expertise allows you the ability to create your own product. For example, a hairdresser could create a "5-Step System for Managing Your Hair Color" and then sell that in a booklet or video format with a product line. No matter the industry, you can figure out a product that you can sell.

Also, an important decision is whether you want to work with businesses or direct consumers. If you have created a new line of baby products, do you want to sell them directly to consumers through a web site or storefront or do you want to develop relationships with resellers of baby products that already have a captive market? Again, this is not an either/or decision. You can sell to both, however, you must be very careful not to undercut your resellers on price if you decide to work with both consumers and resellers.

How to Sell Your Product-Service

In the early stages of creating a product or service it's important to determine who your market will be. More importantly, you need to ask that market if they would purchase your product or service.

This is a critical step many entrepreneurs fail to complete—specifically asking their audience. "The Apprentice" is Donald Trump's hit television series. If you haven't heard of Donald Trump or "The Apprentice," the first thing I would recommend before finishing this booklet is to do some basic research on successful entrepreneurs and see what they have done and had to sacrifice to make it big. Back to "The Apprentice." In the television show, there are two teams of hopeful apprentices vying for a highly coveted position in Donald Trump's organization. The contestants are asked to perform various tasks each week. Naturally, there is a winning team and a losing team. The losing team will have someone "fired" and that person has to pack his bags and leave the show. Every week a brand name company like "Home Depot," "The Gap," or "Pizza Hut," and many others create a project for the two teams to compete in a challenge. Perhaps the interesting thing in the show to take notice of is when one team does market research and the opposing team does not. Donald Trump and his two other colleagues on the show blast the team that doesn't ask questions or do some type of research before they work on their task.

Even more interesting is that in almost every show where one team did research and the other did not, the winning team was the one who conducted research. Meanwhile, entrepreneurs sit at home watching the show, laugh and say "I should be on this show. I know I do research before creating a product. What were they thinking?"

Yet, when you are involved in your own business how often have YOU done the research? In your particular market, how many people are you thinking of targeting to sell your product or service? Have you actually asked their opinion as to whether they will purchase it and at what price?

Conducting market research before you start a business is critical to the future success of your company and financial well-being. Too often entrepreneurs find themselves six months to six years into a project realizing that they have just wasted their time and retirement money trying to sell something no one wanted. The moral of the story is: **DO THE RESEARCH!**

The following are several ways to sell your product or service:

1. Direct Sales- This is where you set up a network marketing company and they sell for you.
2. Wholesale- Wholesale is where to sell to resellers to retail your product.
3. Retail- Retail is where you sell it yourself to the end user the customer.

If you decide to sell it yourself: Online, Door to door, swap meets, brick and mortar, events and so on…

Section Choosing a Business Model

Thanks to technology, there are more business models to choose from than ever before. Today you can start a business part-time or full-time, at home, online or in a brick-and-mortar commercial location!

The key is to choose a business model that fits your Life Plan. This will ensure that you spend the right number of hours each week, take the right level of risk (some models involve more risk than others), are practical in terms of your financial wherewithal, and gain the kind of satisfaction and success you're after.

First off, you have to make a key choice: How much time do you want to devote to your business?

When you go for a full-time business model, you leave behind whatever you were doing previously to commit yourself completely to your startup. When you make this leap, expect to spend more hours working than you ever did working for someone else.

Alternatively, you can start up a business part-time. With this model, you adapt your business to time-consuming obligations you already have, such as your day job, parenting responsibilities or any other activities that would keep you from making your startup your primary focus.

Once you've determined whether you see yourself as a part-time or full-time entrepreneur, consider our list of business model options.

1. Home-based
2. Brick-and-mortar
3. e-Commerce
4. eBay
5. Franchising
6. Licensing your product
7. Multi-level marketing

Section Business Model Options

Home-based Business

Drawing upon technology, you can create a legitimate and competitive business from home. It's part of our culture now, accounting for more than half of all businesses. Home-based businesses can be run full-time or part-time, and may or may not be web-based.

Upside

- **Less risk and lower startup costs** - allows you to test the entrepreneurial waters without having to spend money on real estate and staff.
- **Easily scalable** - you can make your home-based business as big or small as you'd like to suit existing commitments, such as parenthood and a day job.
- **Outsourcing** - a great strategy to keep things simple at home. You can contract with other companies to do your public relations, warehousing, shipping, website management, even manufacturing.

Downside

- Shipping activities and customer traffic at residential properties are restricted by local zoning ordinances (check with your local government for details).
- Working at home can come with lots of distractions and can infringe on your other domestic commitments.
- If foot traffic is necessary in your business, your home may not make the desired impression on customers.

Brick-and-Mortar

This is a business with a classic physical location outside of the home. It involves a dedicated facility - whether retail, wholesale, service or manufacturing.

Upside

- Gives you an **opportunity to work face-to-face** with people and become more involved in your community.
- A **physical location** may attract walk-in traffic to supplement traffic you gain through marketing efforts, depending on your type of business.
- Gives you a **dedicated space** to go to work each day and become mentally and physically immersed in running your business.

Downside

- Higher risk and startup costs (build-out costs to set up your location, lease/purchase costs)
- Requires a full-time commitment upfront to get the facility ready for business, as well as to hire personnel to staff it.
- If your concept is retail-oriented, you must acquire inventory to merchandize your store.

e-Commerce

In this model, you don't have foot traffic in your business, only traffic to your website. You sell your product through your website to consumers or to other businesses.

Upside

- As with a home-based business, this is a **lower risk, lower cost business** to start. You don't necessarily need lots of personnel, inventory and facilities.
- You can choose to do it **full-time or part-time**.
- **Easily scalable** – you can make your e-commerce business as big or small as you'd like to suit existing commitments, such as parenthood and a day job.
- You can tap into a **national, or even global, customer base** through the internet.

Downside

- As with a brick-and-mortar store, shipping, inventory management, and credit card processing can all become headaches if you don't do them right, particularly if you are a one-person show.
- Over 800 million people access the internet globally, but it's a challenge to a) get that traffic to come to your site and b) convert them into a customer confident enough to make a purchase.

eBay

A sub-category of e-commerce, but one big enough to consider on its own, eBay can serve as a location for your online store, and allow you to tap into its huge marketplace.

Upside

- **Lower cost, lower risk** than starting an independent e-commerce site as there are a great many tools to help eBay sellers get their businesses off the ground (e.g. PayPal to accept payment, a ready-made marketplace, online store templates, market research tools).
- Avoid having to build **website traffic** from scratch - eBay has a huge following worldwide, so you tap into a vast existing customer base.

Downside

- As with a brick-and-mortar store, shipping, inventory management, and credit card processing can all become headaches if you don't do them right, particularly if you are a one-person show.
- Even with the guaranteed traffic that eBay offers, you will still face stiff competition from existing sellers who have already staked their claim and built up a strong feedback rating & customer base.

Franchising

When you choose a franchise business model, you use someone else's proven business concept as your entrepreneurial roadmap. Typically you pay an upfront fee, as well as a portion of revenues over time, to the franchisor.

Upside

- **Lower risk** than opening an independent brick-and-mortar business, because franchising provides you with a streamlined process to start your business, as well as support for marketing, business plan samples and estimates, assistance with real estate issues, and staff training.
- Provides you with a **recognized, established brand** to attract customers more quickly.
- To illustrate the lower risk inherent in a franchise, **success rates** for franchises are higher than non-franchise businesses.

Downside

- You've got to be able to pay the upfront franchise fees.
- Franchise guidelines can be strict and limit your ability to get creative with your business.

- Your financial upside is somewhat limited because you must pay your franchisor a cut of your profits.

Resource:

To learn more about franchising options, visit the International Franchise Association.

Licensing your Product

If you're working a day job and don't want to start a business, you can still take advantage of your great product idea by licensing the product to another company that has the entire infrastructure in place to properly manufacture, market and sell the product.

Upside

- **Lower risk** because you can work on your product part-time.
- **Lower cost** because your main expense is production of a prototype and testing the product to make it attractive to potential licensees (rather than the cost involved in setting up an entire business to make, market and sell the product).
- **Freedom** to move on to the next big business idea - if you do successfully license your product idea, you could receive royalties long after you've stopped working on the product!

Downside

- Finding the right licensee takes tenacity and determination, and can take a long time – don't quit your day job!
- Unless your product gets sold in a significant enough volume by the company to which you license it, the amount of royalties you receive can be low or non-existent.
- It's extremely difficult to get through the door of big companies to start a negotiation. That's partly why less than 3% of all patented ideas actually make it to market through licensing agreements.

Multi-level Marketing

Multi-level marketing (MLM) is a marketing and distribution structure. People at the top sell to those below them, who in turn sell to those below them. The higher up you are in this structure, the more money you can make. The challenge with MLM businesses is that people at the top are frequently the winners. The vast majority of people at the bottom end up spending money and time to get involved and end up losing whatever they put in.

If you're determined to choose a business with an MLM model, be sure to check with at least a handful of other people who've entered at your level (who you identify on your own, separate from people the MLM promoter refers you to), and see what they have to say. Find out their perspectives on how - and if it's possible - to be successful.

Upside

- Typically, **limited startup costs** (a membership or initial inventory commitment).
- Viable **home-based business**.
- You are provided **pre-packaged tools, products and sales techniques**.

Downside

- **Most** people lose money in MLM activities, because they can't sell the product as effectively as they thought they could.
- Credibility can become an issue, especially if you start treating friends like they're customers.

Creating the Business Name

Business names are fun to create. I love to sit down and brainstorm ideas for company names. I have also learned a lot about what NOT to do when choosing a name. So here are some basic rules to keep in mind. Also, if you have already decided on a name, you need to look at these rules to make sure your name is clear and easy to understand. We will go into more details in the business plan section of the guide.

1.   Is the name easy to pronounce? Will you have to repeat it every time someone calls your office?

2.   Do a name check in your local area to see if anyone is using the name.

3.   Check the Secretary of State database that no one is using the company name currently.

4.   Complete a National name check with each State and see who is using the company name.

5.   Perform a name search with the Federal Trademark office.

6.   File a trademark on the name/logo with the State and Federal trademark offices.

7.   If using a corporation, you will want an ending for your name that includes one of the following:
   a. Inc.
   b. Incorporated
   c. Corporation
   d. Corp.
   e. Ltd.
   More details in the section named "Business Organization"

8.   Check your state for certain words that may not be allowed without specific licenses or approval such as:
   a. Bank
   b. School
   c. College
   d. Insurance
   e. Real Estate
   f. Medical
   g. Trust

Business Organization

> **OBJECTIVE:** When you have decided which business is right for you, you will have three important decisions to make. In this session you will discover: whether to go into business alone or with a partner; the type of business organization to use; and what professional advisors to select.

Should You Have a Partner?

It is best to make your decision concerning whether to have a partner by preparing a "for" and "against" list. The most common reasons for joining with another person to start the business:

- There is safety in numbers. In other words, you have two heads instead of one to discuss and make decisions. In the words of Solomon: "Two can accomplish more than twice as much as one. If one fails, the other pulls him up; but if a man falls when he is alone, he's in trouble. And one standing alone can be attacked and defeated, but two can stand back-to-back and conquer. Three is even better, for a triple-braided cord is not easily broken."
- You will not need to be at the business at all times. You will have someone else who will be there to share the load and permit you to take a vacation and have sick time.
- You will also have a highly motivated co-worker, not just someone who is earning a paycheck.
- Partners can also be advantageous when they have complementary skills.
- It may be necessary to have a partner to contribute capital and share the risk when things do not proceed as planned.
- A partnership should have provisions made for exit strategies and you will need experts experienced in succession planning. What happens if a partner dies or becomes disabled? Or if family members want to join or quit the firm?

Some of the arguments against having a partner:

- You will have to share the rewards if the business is successful.
- You will lose total control over the business, particularly if you and your partner have difficulty in making decisions.
- You will have to share the recognition that will come if the business is successful.
- A partner can be a disaster if his or her judgment is not good.
- You run the risk of a falling out and perhaps the necessity of one partner buying the other out if dissention arises.

Some of the things to consider in deciding whether a particular person will make a good partner are whether you have similar work habits, similar objectives concerning how to run the business and whether your strong points are similar or complementary. For example, different capabilities permit you to spread the workload and provide better coverage for problems.

Different capabilities may permit you to give each partner a veto over important decisions in his or her area of expertise to help maintain stability and eliminate conflicts. Finally, you may want to consider whether you should have a buy-sell agreement in the event of a disagreement, and how the purchaser will pay for the portion of the business he or she is buying (and whether you should fund the buy-sell agreement with insurance in the event of the death of a partner).

Choosing a Business Structure
What Type of Business Organization is Best for You?

When you first decide to open a company you have a choice to make, do you just go down to the county/city office and fill out a business license application (DBA-Doing Business As is what that stands for), or do you form a corporation or LLC? By going to the city or county offices and applying for a business license you will be asked what form of business you are forming. If you have not filed with the Secretary of State to form a corporation or LLC, you will indicate either a Sole-Proprietorship or General Partnership. The business license application and approval process for the name is sufficient to allow you to run your business. A Sole Proprietorship and General Partnership have some tax benefits for running a small business, most of which you will also find with running a Corporation or LLC. Some tax advisers say you should only operate as Sole Proprietor or General Partnership when you have less than $5,000,000 in annual revenue. There is less paperwork to deal with, you get the tax benefits of a small business, and you don't have to file a separate tax return. The one area the tax professional is not looking at is the liability aspects of running a small business. Yes, you can get liability insurance, however, the premiums in many cases don't justify the cost versus the small fee to incorporate. To operate your company as a Corporation or Limited Liability Company (LLC), you will need to file paperwork with the Secretary of State in which you want to operate. There are many advantages to incorporating as we will discuss. A comparison of some of the most common business entities is below.

Sole Proprietorships and General Partnerships
A sole proprietorship and a general partnership are the simplest and least expensive forms of businesses. If you currently operate a small business on your own and report your business income on Schedule C, then you are a sole proprietorship – it's that easy. A general partnership is automatically created when two or more people go into business together. Because of this simplicity, most businesses are sole proprietorships or general partnerships. However, even with low start-up costs and ease of operation, other factors can make these the *most expensive* business structures in the long run. First, your liability for business debts is **unlimited**. These entities cannot shield you, as the owner, from liabilities that could literally cost you and your family everything. For instance, if you have significant business losses or an adverse legal judgment, creditors can force you to sell your home and personal property to cover the claim.
Second, you may be hurting yourself tax-wise since corporations have a variety of tax advantages, such as the ability to reduce self-employment taxes. Furthermore, there are no business entities more highly scrutinized by the IRS than sole proprietorships. Finally, when it comes time to selling or passing on your sole proprietorship, it can be tedious.

The Best Time to Incorporate

The best time to incorporate for almost any business owner is when:

• You first start the company or when an existing company has over $45,000 in annual revenue.

The company operates in a highly litigious industry. For example, construction, consulting etc.

- You want to take advantage of the many tax benefits of a corporation.

- You want to take advantage of the following benefits of the corporate structure

- Limit personal liability of officers and owners

- Protection of personal assets from the business

- Protection of corporate assets from the owners and officers

- Build a separate business credit profile

- Raise capital easier

- Solicit investors easier

- Lower your tax liability

- Develop a strong corporate image

- Lower the risk of a tax audit

Corporations
What is a Corporation?

Although a corporation is separate and distinct from its stockholders, directors or officers, it is a separate entity that can act only through its members, officers, or agents and cannot have knowledge or belief of any subject independent of the knowledge or belief of its people. A stockholder (owner or partial owner) is a holder of shares of stock in the corporation and is NOT IN LEGAL DANGER for the acts of the corporation. In other words, you, as the owner, are not responsible. A stockholder is not the employer of those working for the corporation nor is he the owner of corporate property.

A corporation is a citizen in the state wherein it was created and does not cease to be a citizen of its state of domicile by engaging in business or acquiring property in another state. Since corporations are solely creatures of Statute, their powers are derived from the constitution and laws of the state in which it is incorporated. As an artificial person, a corporation is considered to have its domicile in the state where it is incorporated and the place where it has a statutory presence. When the corporation functions in a different state, the site of its designated resident or registered agent is sometimes called its "statutory domicile."

The existence of the corporation is not affected by the death or bankruptcy of a shareholder, officer, or director. It has a continuous existence as long as it complies with the statutory requirements of the state where it is incorporated.

For the purposes of raising capital and building credit for a small to medium sized business, corporations provide the best chances for gaining approval and are recommended. A corporation is a separate legal entity from the owners and officers of the business. It files a SS-4 form with the Internal Revenue Service to obtain a tax identification number that will be used to file taxes and can be used to create the company's own credit profile. Corporations are the oldest business entity in the United States and have the most case histories.

Credit card companies have designed credit cards just for corporations. Venture capitalists and banks will spend more time with the owners of a corporation than that of a sole proprietorship. Corporations are taken more seriously in business. Some companies will not hire another business unless it is incorporated.

There are several types of corporations, but the two that are most commonly used are the "S" and "C."

To decide which of the two is best for your situation, consult a tax professional.

Which Entity to Choose

The S Corporation should be considered:
- When the owners live in a state with no personal state income tax
- Have one or two individuals who own the company (Can be as many as 35)
- Have sales less than $250,000

The C Corporation should be considered:
- When the owners live outside the country
- When the owners live in a state with a state income tax
- When several individuals are involved in ownership
- When other entities are involved in ownership
- Have sales greater than $60,000

When to use a Limited Liability Company - LLC
- Any partnership
- Owning real estate for investment purposes
- Have several entities that own the business

Advantages of Incorporating Your Business

If you're a business owner, you need to protect your personal assets. Incorporating your business, or forming an LLC, are two of the best ways to do just that. In addition, the corporate
business structure can save you money in taxes, give you greater business flexibility and make it easier for you to raise capital.

Paying taxes is not fun, so why pay more than you have to? You may have heard that incorporating your business can help you save thousands of dollars in taxes. It's true. Even if your corporation has just one employee (yourself), you can still enjoy significant tax savings.

Just as important, you will have peace of mind, knowing that your personal assets are protected from business liabilities.

For example, if John Smith has a consulting business that he operates as a sole proprietorship, the company name is John Smith; however, he could file a DBA to have the business known as Smith's Consulting. Corporations, limited liability companies (LLCs) and other state-formed business entities can also file DBAs to transact business using a name other than the name included on their state formation documents.

To learn which business licenses may be necessary for your particular business, you can contact the appropriate state and local agencies to inquire about requirements and application procedures. There are also services that can research business license requirements for you and provide you with the necessary forms and application instructions.

As a new business owner, you'll want to ensure your business is starting on the right foot by complying with all the laws and ordinances governing your type of business and location.

Once brought to life by filing Articles of Incorporation with the state, a corporation can act much like a person. It can own and operate a business, hire employees, buy and sell goods and services, enter into contracts, lease or buy real estate, maintain its own checking and savings accounts, and sue and be sued. A corporation is not affected by the death or bankruptcy of any shareholder, officer or director. Instead, it continues to exist as long as it complies with the state requirements and corporate formalities.

You may have heard of the term "S-corporation" and "C-corporation." They are actually both the same type business entity, but an S-corporation has simply made a special IRS election to be

*"Sole Proprietorships can become the most
expensive type of entity in the long run."*

treated as a pass-through entity for tax purposes, much like a sole proprietorship or partnership. In other words, corporate profits "pass through" to the owners, who pay taxes on the profits at their individual tax rates. C-corporations, on the other hand, are traditional corporations with two potential levels of tax. A C-corporation pays tax on its corporate income (the first tax). Then, if a C-corporation distributes profits to its stockholders, the stockholders pay personal income tax on those dividends (the second tax). Although this may seem like a significant disadvantage, C-corporations actually have greater tax flexibility than S-corporations and can easily minimize any "double taxation" problems.

The S Corporation

For years, CPAs and attorneys across the country have been recommending that small business owners operate their company as an S Corporation. Depending on your specific case, you may want to consider this type of business entity.
One consideration to look at is the issue of double taxation. S Corporations allow the profits and losses of a corporation to flow directly through to the owners/shareholders of the corporation. All of this takes place without taxation at the corporate level. This eliminates the potential for double taxation.
Double taxation of a C Corporation occurs when the corporation has its profits taxed initially, and then the dividends paid out to shareholders are taxed again on the personal level.
There are certain qualifications that the corporation must meet in order to elect S Corporation status.

1.   It must be a domestic corporation formed in the USA.
2.   It may have no more than 100 shareholders.
3.   It may only have individuals, estates or certain trusts as shareholders.
4.   It may not have nonresident alien shareholders.
5.   It may only have one class of stock.
6.   It must be a small business corporation (financial institutions such as banks, insurance companies, building and loan associations or mutual savings and loan associations cannot take advantage of electing S Corporation).
7.   It must conform to state statutory restrictions, which limit the transfer of shares/ownership, of the company.

An S Corporation operates on a December 31st calendar year ending. However, as with most rules, there are exceptions. The corporation can make a Section 444 election, which generally allows for a tax year ending September 30, October 31, or November 30, but estimated tax payments must be made that would offset any advantage a shareholder might gain by having an offsetting fiscal year.

Considerations When Electing an S Corporation:
    1.   When losses flow through the corporation, those losses can be used to offset ACTIVE income from either spouse (active income includes income derived directly from business activity).
    2.   If the S Corporation earns ACTIVE PROFITS they can be offset by losses from other businesses and/or operating expenses from a sole proprietorship.
    3.   There is no double taxation.

4. There are no penalties for excessive accumulated earnings for S Corporations.

5. The S Corporation shareholder/employee may only deduct 25% of the cost of medical insurance as adjustment to income.

6. The S Corporation must report paid premiums for health premiums and group term life insurance as taxable income if the shareholder owns more than 2% of the stock.

The LLC – Limited Liability Company

Limited Liability Companies (LLC) have been around for many years in such countries as South

America and Germany. The LLC first came to America in 1977 in Wyoming. Evidence of LLC legislation in other states around the country did not take place until the IRS made a key ruling on the taxation of this new structure. On September 19, 1998, the IRS issued Revenue Ruling 88-76, stating that LLCs would be taxed as partnerships even though none of the members (partners) or managers would be personally liable for any of the company's debt. This ruling encouraged other states to adopt this new vehicle as well. Now, all states have accepted LLCs into their domain as legitimate business structures.

The LLC structure is commonly used for holding real estate. One reason is that LLC structures are similar to partnerships, limited partnerships, S Corporations, and trusts. An LLC is a flow through entity. It passes all of the LLC profits and losses directly to the members of the LLC. Individual members are therefore taxed at their personal income tax rates.

An LLC can also be handy when exploring joint ventures. For example, let's say you are enjoying the benefits of controlling your own corporation, and you now want to combine efforts with another individual by forming a joint venture. If each company was a corporation, you could form a separate LLC and have the members (owners) be the two current corporations. This way you don't have to disrupt your current businesses and will be able to run those businesses exactly how you want without the other person getting involved. This is a simple way to bring two corporate entities together and keep at arm's length from the business at hand.

Which State to Choose
Where Should I Form My Corporation or LLC?

Most people choose to form their corporation or LLC in their home state because it's the easiest and often the most cost-effective. If you incorporate in a different state, you often need to register as a "foreign corporation" in your home state, which requires a separate filing fee and subjects you to your home state's taxes. In addition, you can save money by serving as your own registered agent. There are several promoters of incorporating; in two particular states, **Delaware and Nevada.**

Delaware is home to over 55% of every publicly traded company in the United States. Delaware has the oldest case history for corporations and from an early stage in U.S. history made an effort to be business friendly. State Statutes are laws created by a state's Congress and House of Representatives. These Statutes, among other things, have requirements for how a corporation must be run in order to keep the benefits and protections a corporation or LLC provides. In the state of Delaware, the state Statutes were written to protect the shareholders of corporations in case the company was sued. In fact, Delaware created a Chancellery Court, a separate court system for businesses and has accumulated over 200 years of court decisions. With the long history of court cases and state statutes protection, the shareholders even more than most states, find the majority of public companies incorporated in Delaware and then filed to do business in another state.

If you choose to incorporate in one state and then decide to operate your company in another, you will have to Foreign File your company in the new state. So, if you incorporate in Delaware but have your office in Oregon, you need to file all the fees in Delaware, have a Resident Agent in Delaware, and then pay fees to Oregon to operate in Oregon as a Foreign Corporation. The Foreign Corporation status is for companies from one state operating in another. A Corporation from another country would be referred to as an Alien Corporation. The State of Nevada's politicians decided a few years ago to diversify the state's income; they wanted something more than just gaming taxing. So they decided to change the state Statutes to similar wording as Delaware's when it came to Corporations and LLCs. The Statutes went one step further to write specific law to protect the Directors and Officers of a company even more than they already were.

Today, Nevada has a significant number of corporations formed by out of state businesses, who file back in their home states, just to take advantage of the protections Nevada law offers.

So, which state do you choose? If you want to go public some day, choose Delaware, otherwise stay in your home state. The cost of filing a corporation in a state, other than the one you are doing business in and then having to foreign file back in your home state is just not cost effective in most cases.

If you maintain corporate requirements in your home state, you will have just as much protection as Nevada and Delaware have anyway.

Delaware, Wyoming, New Mexico, Nevada and Other "Business-Friendly" States

If your home state has a high corporate income tax or high state fee, and your corporation will not "do business" in your home state, it may be wise to incorporate in a tax-free state. Nevada does not have a state income tax, and Delaware does not tax out-of-state business activities.

Typically, this strategy works best with companies that have offices in multiple states, or with passive investment companies. "Doing business" means more than just selling products or making passive investments. It usually requires occupying an office or otherwise having an active business presence. Furthermore, by incorporating in a different state, your corporation becomes subject to the corporate laws of that state. Delaware and Nevada are known for their business-friendly laws and courts. While it is possible to reduce your taxes through this method, we recommend that you to consult with a tax adviser to see if it is appropriate for your business. Finance Builders can help you form a corporation or LLC in all 50 states.

Wyoming is unique; in that, the corporation can be domiciled in Wyoming as if it was there the entire time. It's a continuance of the corporate presence. This means a corporation in the Bahamas, New York, or anywhere else, is continued in Wyoming as if it has always existed there.

Nevada corporations are more popular--simply because there are more people selling them. There are more professionals, incorporators and nominee officers selling Nevada aged corporations. Nevada is a great place to incorporate because the state of Nevada is so business friendly. In comparison, Wyoming is just as business-friendly and costs less than Nevada. Wyoming has fewer promoters of incorporation services, by nature of their state population (500,000 people). It stands to reason that by the mere numbers of Nevada's promoters, and their marketing skills, that there is much more publicity about Nevada corporations. Wyoming corporations are just as better (and cost less). Why are they better?

In Wyoming, no business license is required.

In Nevada a business license is required by the State of Nevada (not the Nevada Secretary of State), which requires the owners' names, address, SSN's, and DOB's.

- Wyoming annual filing fees are $50 per year. In Nevada, filing fees are $225 per year.
- Wyoming's corporate code was written with the Constitution and property rights in mind for the small business person. Wyoming is known for hunting, fishing, ranching and the defense industry.

- Nevada's corporate code was written to protect the casino's, the brothels and organized crime. Nevada is known for gambling, prostitution, slick business and fast times. The audit rate for Nevada companies is four times higher than any other state in the USA.
- Wyoming is in the black with no income tax.
- Nevada is in the red, with no end in sight, and there's no income tax for the moment.
- Wyoming filing fees are going to stay the same.
- Nevada filing fees will go up.

NEVADA

Effective June 1, 2005, Nevada requires the filing of an annual business license, whether or not you do business in Nevada. This business license mandates the name, addresses, social security numbers and the ownership percentages of each identified stockholder.

The dangerous part is that many Nevada resident agents are not talking about this requirement because they know of the negative impact it'll have on their business. This means that your ability to maintain the corporate veil and to obtain corporate credit is affected if you're not in compliance by failing to file the Nevada business license.

NEVADA CLAIMS THEY DON'T HAVE AN INFORMATION SHARING AGREEMENT WITH THE IRS. THIS IS MISLEADING.

This information collected in Nevada, although not automatically shared with the IRS, is accessible through a subpoena or court order. In addition, the Nevada Secretary of State admits to **SELLING** their information to database companies, like ChoicePoint. And ChoicePoint sells information to the IRS. Why claim to provide a level of privacy that doesn't exist? They want to sell companies, even if their representation is misleading.

Nevada privacy is meaningless at this point.

NEW MEXICO LLC

For start-up companies on a budget, we offer a new solution to those looking for an economical shelf company. We're always looking for ways to sell companies for less.

New Mexico offers several positive attributes:

No annual fee to the state.

Most states require an annual fee. NM is the only state that doesn't require one for LLC's. We don't know how long this will last.

No need for annual reporting to the state of NM.

Disadvantages:

Wait two weeks for the documents

If you're in a hurry to obtain a certificate of good standing or certified copy of the articles, you may wait up to three weeks.

So, if you can wait a few weeks for the docs, it's a good buy. If you're in a hurry, choose Wyoming. In contrast, Wyoming allows for you to download and print the certificate of good standing. Wyoming is great when you're rushed to do a job. We've compensated for the wait by ordering the NM Certificates in advance and in keeping them on file. But if you need more of them, you're still waiting another two to three weeks. Think about what is more important to you and choose accordingly.

What about Delaware? Do we offer Delaware shelf companies?
No. Delaware is best for going public with an initial offering. So, if you're heading off to be another Amazon.com or IBM, go with Delaware. Otherwise, small business is best served from Wyoming. New Mexico comes in at a close second because they cost less.

After Your Corporation is formed

Celebrate!
Just so you know every state has a requirement that you maintain specific documents for your corporation each year and file yearly fees. In every state there has been case law that shows owners of businesses (Statement of Information), who failed to maintain these corporate records and had their personal assets at risk because the corporation was deemed invalid.
I hear it often. "I thought a corporation was there to protect my personal life no matter what." Well, sorry to those dreamers who feel this way. It's just like the saying, "There is no free lunch."
To me, it makes sense. If you are going to form a corporation and want the protections and tax savings the corporation provides, you must do something in order to maintain those privileges. Just like any relationship; marriage, children, friends, employees – you have to work at keeping the relationship strong. It doesn't just happen automatically because you happen to get married or have a child.

With a corporation, the key areas that you need to maintain in most every state are:
- Annual Meeting Minutes of the Shareholders
- Stock Ledger and Stock Certificates Issued with Shares to Each Shareholder
- Resolutions that Track the Activities of the Corporation
- Statement of Information updates

Most business owners understand the need for these items, but aren't sure how to track them or put them together. Our business development company Biz Help 101 has all those forms as well as we can assist you is setting up your corporation. On our online community is the entire how to's as well for you to do it yourself.

The Corporate Structure

A corporation is made up of a few key documents. These documents determine the laws, guidelines, procedures and format of how a corporation/LLC is put together, operated and dissolved. These documents are:

State Statutes – Laws developed by each state that govern how a corporation or LLC can operate in their state.

Articles of Incorporation – The document that is filed with the Secretary of State in order to form the corporation. It indicates the name of the company, number of shares, etc.

Articles of Organization – It is the LLC's Articles of Incorporation.
Bylaws – The bylaws in most states do not need to be filed with the Secretary of State. The bylaws are the corporation's requirements for running the business. It says what officers there will be, how they are elected, when meetings will be held and how voting of the shareholders will take place, to name just a few of the items.

Operating Agreement – This is the LLC's Bylaws.

Officer List – An annual list of officers must be filed with the Secretary of State indicating the names of the officers of the company. This is required for LLCs and Corporations.

Stock Ledger – The stock ledger is where all names of shareholders must be recorded. Each transaction of a stock certificate is written down in this booklet.

Stock Certificates – The Corporation's paper that represents the number of shares owned by the shareholder written on the Certificate.

Certificates of Ownership – The LLC's paper that represents the percentage of ownership by the members of the company.

Resolution – A resolution is a written document that provides permission for a corporation to perform a specific task. The permission is granted by either a Director or Officer depending on the activity.

The One Person Corporation

The diagram below provides the traditional corporate structure. Regardless if you have 1,000 employees or the company is just you, maintaining this structure will be critical to the success of your business.

Too often entrepreneurs do not see themselves as a Shareholder of their company, yet they frequently say they are the owner. By running your business from the Shareholder's perspective you need to step away from the Officer, Manager, and Employee mentality.

There are a few questions all entrepreneurs must ask themselves to better understand how to separate the shareholder, the director, officer, manager and employee even when they are all the same person. The questions are:

- Am I earning a consistent salary from the business?
- Could I earn a greater salary working for someone?
- Is the company creating equity? Is it worth more each year?
- If I were just an investor looking at this business, would I invest?
- If I did invest in the business, am I happy with my return on investment?
- As a shareholder, am I happy with the decisions the officers and managers are making?
- As a shareholder, am I happy with each employee I have?
- If I invested my money that I put into this company somewhere else, would I have received a better return?
- If I invested my time with another company would I have received a better return?

Each of these questions forces you to start thinking about how you should operate your company from the shareholder point of view, not a mixed viewpoint of a manager, shareholder and officer.

The Corporate Structure as outlined by most states is:

Shareholders
- Owners of the corporation
- They elect the Board of Directors
- Do not possess power in daily decisions

Directors
- Elected by Shareholders to serve one-year terms
- Create the long-term goals and policies
- Not involved in daily activities
- Appoint and Remove Officers

Officers
- Appointed by the Board of Directors
- Supervises Management

Management
- Supervise Daily Operations
- Hire Employees

Employees
- Perform daily systems and policies of the company

The LLC Structure as outlined by most states is:

Members
- Owners of the corporation
- Do not possess power in daily decisions
- Similar to Shareholders in a Corporate Structure

Managers
- Create the long-term goals and policies
- Not involved in daily activities
- Appoint and Remove Management

Management
- Supervise Daily Operations
- Hire Employees

Employees
- Perform daily systems and policies of the company.
  The purchase of "resident agent services" is often required by many
  incorporating companies. A resident agent is as simple as an address for
  legal process. In other words, as a corporation or LLC you need to have a
  physical address that you can accept mail and courier deliveries during

normal business hours, Monday – Friday 9:00 a.m. to 5:00 p.m. You can use your own business address. You do not need to pay an annual fee of $100 or more to have someone perform this service for you. The only real benefit of using a resident agent service is if you are incorporated in a state that you don't have a physical location.

Obviously there are variations in these rules, and you should consult with your attorney and/or accountant in each specific case to determine what form of organization best fits your needs.

One of the things to consider in making the final decision is, although a corporation has limited liability for its shareholders, if the corporation does not have sufficient assets various creditors may insist on personal guarantees from the shareholders. Examples are your landlord, some suppliers, and by law, liability for certain payroll taxes and liabilities to employees.

Laws That May Affect You

There are many laws that are applicable to owners of small businesses. It is best to consult with professionals to determine which laws will be applicable to you, what permits you will need to commence business and where to go to comply with the various rules. Your attorney should be able to assist you in complying with labor laws such as the employment of minors, illegal aliens and workplace safety rules.

Your accountant should be able to assist you in filing:

- **Income tax returns**
- **Franchise tax returns**
- **Employment tax returns**
- **The time for payment of withheld and employers share of employment taxes**
- **Unemployment tax returns and payment**

Sales Tax Reports and Payments Take a look at our Small Business Tax Center created in association with the I.R.S.

Your attorney may be able to help with requirements for business licenses, including special licenses for particular businesses as well as building codes and permits for remodeling and zoning laws, health department requirements and environmental laws.

How Can Your Professionals Help You?

Your Attorney

In addition to the above items, your attorney should draw your partnership agreement or form your corporation, including the issuance of stock and appropriate filings with the Secretary of State and the Department of Corporations. He or she will help advise on the best form of ownership, assist in negotiations to buy an existing business and review documents if you are buying a franchise. He or she will also advise on buy-sell agreements and draft appropriate documents.

If your business will require renting an office, store or factory, your attorney should review and approve your lease document. A lease obligation can become your biggest liability, and your attorney can help negotiate fair and protective terms. For example, if you anticipate growth, your lease should include a provision for how expansion requirements will be handled.

Your new business may require specialized legal advice to establish and protect your intellectual property rights. Intellectual property includes your ownership rights to your business name, trademarks, copyrights and patents. Intellectual property law is a specialized field, and you may need an attorney who specializes in these matters.

Your Accountant

Your accountant can be an important advisor in start-up decisions, such as

- Deciding the appropriate division of the capital you contribute to a corporation between stock and loans.
- Determining the best form of ownership.
- Helping set up the books and records of the business.
- Advising computer needs for accounting purposes.
- Filing tax returns, advising on compensation of owners, preparing financial statements, helping forecast cash needs, including whether to expand, addition of employees and determining profitability.

He or she will have a continuing role in filing tax returns, advising on compensation of owners, preparing financial statements, helping forecast cash needs, including whether to expand, addition of employees, and whether you are really making money in this venture.

You will need to decide with your accountant what kind of financial statements are prepared. There are several audit levels that are described in our session one "Getting financial controls in place" in the Building My Own Business course.

Your Payroll Service Provider

All entrepreneurs face the dreaded question, "How am I ever going to handle my payroll, payroll taxes and comply with ever-changing state and federal laws?"

Thanks to efficiencies achieved through computer technologies, a huge industry has emerged to take over increasingly complex payroll issues. "Payroll Service Providers" now permit small businesses to outsource these functions at very low costs. Now the start-up entrepreneur, even with a payroll of one person, can "outsource" his or her Human Resources department.

There are many payroll service providers listed in the Yellow Pages and on the Internet (go to "payroll service providers" on search engines.) In recent years, payroll service providers have expanded their services to handle other personnel issues as well, such as managing retirement plans, workers compensation insurance and pre-employment verification. Many payroll service providers incorporate services such as

- 401K and Simple IRA
- Business Tax Protection & Payment
- Health Insurance
- Human Resources Help Desk
- Human Resources Software
- New Hire Reporting
- Pay-by-Pay Workers Compensation Insurance

- Payroll Tax Calculation, Deposit and Filing
- Pre-Employment Screening/Background Checks
- Reporting Solutions
- State Unemployment Insurance Management
- Time and Attendance Solutions

Your Pension Plan Manager

As a business owner, you can participate in the benefits of tax-deferred pension plans for yourself and your employees. Good pension planning will help you attract and keep good employees. Some payroll service providers now handle pension plan management.

Your professionals can also be of significant assistance in helping formulate your business plan by advising on

- The appropriate form of organization.
- Roles of each partner, such as the control of each party.
- The areas in which each will have primary responsibility and the ownership of each party.

In connection with the acquisition of an existing business, they should advise on good and bad terms of the proposed deal and help negotiate with the seller and his or her attorney.

Finally, they should advise on your need for capital, both at the inception of the business and what additional capital will be needed if the business is successful and you decide to expand.

Your Pre-employment Screening Service

Pre-employment screening is especially important when you are starting because you don't have ongoing revenues to offset mistakes. Many start-ups skip screening because they're unfamiliar with it or don't know how to have it done at a reasonable cost. Unfortunately, this can open them up to resume fraud among other undesirable possibilities. A good example of a reputable and inexpensive source for conducting background checks is Employee Screen IQ. (Make sure to use this form to get $25 off for MOBI users). Also, many tips on how to go about the hiring process can be found through search engines by entering "hiring tips."

Consider Outsourcing

As an entrepreneur, your time should be focused on building up your business. A good way to do this is to outsource all the administrative and specialist tasks to external professionals. We recommend using a service like BPOVIA to help with this.

Suggested Activities

- Before you start up, collect referrals to and references about lawyers, accountants and insurance agents so you can select the most appropriate professional advisors well before the time you will need their services. Perhaps they will provide you with initial free consultations for considering them as members of your professional team.

Location, Location, Location

Whether you are a moonlight or full-time entrepreneur, at some time real estate issues will become important to you. The success or failure of most retail businesses will hinge on the owner's selectivity and judgment in selecting the right location.

An initial step in business is selecting where you will live and where your business will be located. You may have the opportunity to relocate to an area where you would really enjoy living and working.

If you are planning to become a franchisor of your business, successful real estate development and precise location criteria for your franchised locations will become key factors in your success. See our session 10 on Franchising Your Business in the Building My Own Business Course.

Zoning Categories

Every city has a planning department at City Hall. You will be dealing with this and other municipal departments and agencies that have discretionary authority to approve or disapprove your intended plans.

You can no longer rely on zoning codes to determine what the rules are in your desired location. Your intended location will often be subject to "precise plan" approval, an environmental impact assessment, and other regulatory issues.

You may find yourself appearing before a review board that can often seem unreasonable in its decisions. Many cities have redevelopment agencies authorized to impose conditions even more stringent than those established by local codes.

One shopping center developer was so frustrated with the demands of city agencies that he finally threw up his hands and sold off his rights to the property. The new owner succeeded in developing the property. His secret, "I went into City Hall and told them that I would do anything they wanted me to do-----and did it."

Now, obviously there will be times when unreasonable conditions will make a location for your business unattractive. In such cases, you should unemotionally look for another location.

Criteria for Home-Based Businesses
Be sure your home business is permitted and you have the license required by the city. Many homes have an association with regulations for the owners. Check to ensure you are in compliance. See our home based business session for those considering operating a business from their home.

Criteria for a Manufacturing, Warehousing, or Industrial Business

- Room for future expansion
- Convenient for employees
- Good Accessibility
- Available labor force
- Appropriate utilities
- Convenient to freight and express delivery systems

Criteria for a Retail Business
Each retail and commercial business has its own criteria. For example, a donut shop should be located on the "going-to-work" side of the street. On the other

hand, a liquor store should be on the side of the street with traffic going home from work.

The selection of your first location will have an overwhelming impact on your chances for success.

In Session 1, you analyzed businesses that are similar to the one you chose. Did you analyze where they were located and why?

- Select the appropriate type of center (mall, strip, mini). Some business do best in a large center but some, like Mini-Marts, video stores and Laundromats, do better in much smaller centers. Others such as florist, nursery or antique stores, do well located on the street front.
- Demographic data will provide you information about the neighborhood. It will inform you about the population, the number of households, estimated population by race, age and income level within a one, two or five-mile radius. You can find firms that supply this information on the Internet. A good place to start is the International Council of Shopping Centers at www.icsc.org.
- Walk and talk the area. You will be surprised how much you can learn by talking to customers, employees and owners.
- Traffic count is very important because it will give you the number of cars at the intersection. You can also get the pedestrian count, which is great for drop-in or walk-in business. This report can be obtained from the local traffic department.
- Visibility and signage: Customers must know you are there. They should be able to see your store. Usually the end or corner location is better, which is why the rent for those spaces is higher. Get the biggest sign you can. Tell the public clearly what you are selling. Examples: Travel, Gifts, Pets, tell the products. Both your lease and the city ordinances will have limitations regarding your signs.
- Access and parking: Be sure you have adequate and convenient parking. Avoid streets with dividers or one-way traffic. Customers prefer stores where the parking is in the front.
- Proximity to competition: Know where your competitors are located. You can get the names and address from the Yellow Pages. Find out what your competition is doing and how they are doing it.
- Generators (anchors): These are the big national stores in a mall or shopping center. For example, Albertson's, Nordstrom, Wal-Mart and/or McDonald's will help to bring customers into the center. The closer your business can be to generators, the better it usually is for your business.

Searching for a Property

The Internet is a good place to start looking for available properties. You want to partner with experienced agents that are familiar with the geography you're interested in and who know the market. Start your search with a free service like Office Finder, which will link you with the right agents.

Leasing Checklist

- Retain a real estate lawyer to assist you in negotiating your lease or purchase. A five-year lease on a $1,000 per month space is $60,000 (probably a personal obligation) and may well be your largest obligation for your beginning business.
- Most retail stores leases are Net, Net, Net (NNN) leases (a.k.a., Triple Net Lease) meaning that you as tenant will pay for the taxes, insurance, gardening, utilities, security, trash and sewer, litter, graffiti removal and repairs. This charge is based on the square footage of your space. CAM (Common Area Maintenance) charges can be costly so find out the estimated cost per month before signing the lease. CAM charges can vary but will normally include parking lot sweeping and repair and all aspects of common area upkeep.
- Ask for options. At the end of your base term, you can then renew the lease or move. Try to keep your initial term short. There are some compelling reasons to have a short-term lease with options:

  Your business may not be successful at your initial location. A short-term lease will minimize your overall rent obligation.

  You need flexibility in lease terms to accommodate growth. Start-up businesses frequently find that their growth rate is more rapid than expected.

- Consider the possibility that you need to expand your business and will need more space. To provide for this, your lease could provide that if you need more room, your space can be expanded, you can move to another location in the center or you can cancel your lease.
- Don't hurry your decision. There is no such thing as the last good location.
- Don't judge entirely on rent. Pay fair rent for an outstanding location. Don't let the leaser dictate all the lease terms.
- An Internet marketing tool is now available to enable you to locate potential competitors: the "local" link on search engines. To demonstrate the power of this tool, go to a search engine such as Google or Yahoo and enter the type of business you plan to start. Then, click on the "local" link at the top of the page and enter you zip code. Presto: your local competition will be displayed on a map along with links to their Web sites.

Points to Consider Before Signing a Lease or Purchasing Property

- Is the location the best available in the area where you want to be?
- Does it meet your own specific criteria?
- Are utilities and tenant improvements adequate?

Basic Lease Provisions:

Rent: Is the rent comparable to other rents in the same location?

Term: Is your lease for a short-term (a year or less) or long-term?

Floor area: How much square footage of the space? Rent and CAM charges are based on the square footage of your space.

Common area maintenance charges (CAM): What are the estimated charges for a year?

Options: Do you have options to renew the lease after the first term expires?

Rent increase: Is it a fixed rent increase or is it based on the CPI (Consumer Price Index). If CPI, negotiate a percentage cap.

Percentage rent: Some landlords will ask for fixed rent plus a percentage (of your sales) rent. This is an issue to negotiate.

Tenant improvements: Put the agreement in writing as to the responsibilities of the landlord and your responsibilities to do the necessary improvements to get the space open for business. Landlord's Construction Exhibit "C" should be made a part of the lease. Please refer to the sample exhibit furnished in this session.

Right to assign or sublet: Landlord's consent "not to be unreasonably withheld."

Signs: Be specific with exhibit and description.

Provision for expansion requirements: If you think your business will be expanding, make provisions in your lease to provide for anticipated future needs.

Parking rights: Be sure that adequate parking space is provided. In most retail centers, tenants share "common area parking" rights. Nearby restaurants or theaters can monopolize the parking spaces you require.

Personal guarantee: You should avoid this, if possible. If it is required, ask your lawyer to review this clause carefully.

Exclusive: Ask that no other business similar to yours be allowed in the center if it's appropriate.

All leases have Exhibits

Which includes but not excluding:

1. Site plan, which is a drawing of the inside of the store, restrooms, windows, doors, A/C vents and utilities.
2. Sign criteria, put in a drawing of the type of sign you want, be sure to state color and size.
3. Construction obligations: state exactly what the landlord will do and what you will do.
4. Special requirements of tenant

To Rent or to Buy Considerations

- For start-ups, the primary consideration is that capital is needed for the business.
- Are requirements going to change? If so, renting is probably preferable.
- Are there tax or borrowing incentives available if you buy?
- Some make more on the real estate than on the business. Talk to the Community Development Department.
- Ownership fixes future cost and availability of the location.

Do Your Homework

- Completely fill out a standard lease form with contingencies necessary for your particular business.
- Attend local Chamber of Commerce meetings to find out about community opportunities and concerns.
- Fully evaluate a specific location, including the completion of a "Site Criteria" table.
- Maintain contact with the community development department.
- Find and get to know a good real estate lawyer.
- Negotiate an actual lease as a dry-run practice.

Site Location Criteria

You can create your own "Site Model" in order to maintain objectivity when evaluating locations for your business. This can be done by assigning different values to the factors that are most important for your particular business. Then each location can be evaluated against these measurements.

Real estate dealmakers concerned with buying, selling or leasing all require possession of expert negotiating skills. Since it has been determined that negotiating is a learned skill and not a natural one, our session "Develop Negotiating Skills" in BizHelp101.com is recommended.

Some things to keep in mind in site selection:

- There's no such thing as the "last good location."
- Copycatting your most successful competitor's site criteria can help you avoid making mistakes.
- If you are building a chain of stores, never sign a lease on your second location until your first location is profitable and proven.
- It is better to pay fair rent on a great location than pay great rent on a fair location.
- Don't rely on leasing agents to make your site decisions.
- Driving streets and walking neighborhoods is a good way to scout for locations.

The following form will give you a methodical approach for evaluating the strengths and weaknesses of each potential location.

First, evaluate your site location for each factor on a scale of 1 to 10, Number 10 being the highest.

Second, decide the importance of each factor to your particular business on a scale of 1 to 5, Number 5 being the most important.

Multiply the grade by the weight to determine the points for each factor. Add up the points to get a total score. Repeat this process for each site to gain an objective, comparative analysis.

Site Criteria Table			
Factors	**Grade 1-10**	**Weight 1-5**	**Points**
Traffic count: Cars or pedestrians			
Visibility access			
Proximity to competition			
Zoning			
Parking (include off-street parking)			
Condition of premises			
Proximity to customer generators			
Income level of neighborhood			
Population density			
Ethnic make up of neighborhood			
Age factor			
Directional growth of area			
Area improving or deteriorating			
Crime/shoplifting rates			
Availability of qualified employees			
Labor rates of pay			
Supplier proximity			
Terms and rental rates			
Adequacy of utilities, gas, & water			
Transportation accessibility			
		Total Points	

Hiring a professional Web Site Developer

Before hiring a Web developer, it's important to determine

- The purpose and budget of your Web site, as well as the ongoing maintenance needs.
- Who will provide the content and who will own the copyrights for these materials.
- Whether the developer will be responsible for both design and marketing of your Web site.

Look at other Web sites the developer has created and ask for references. Did the developer deliver the product in a timely manner at the quoted price? Did the developer listen effectively and present a product that matched the company's vision?

Once you've identified your developer, get a written contract that specifies the responsibilities of the developer, the timelines for project completion and a complete budget for the total project. This should include arrangements for ongoing maintenance of the site. Keep in mind the developer you choose is someone you will most likely have a long-term relationship with as you add and improve the Web site.

Contracting out your Web site offers several advantages. A professional developer has the technical knowledge to create a site that works with all browsers and should be fluent with the current technologies. Investing in a professional developer will allow you to spend more time on creating a successful business and less time learning the new trade of being your own Web site developer.

Setting Up a Website

Before you get started you need to answer the following questions:

- What types of customers will you attract?
- How will these customers interact with your Web site, and how can you make your Web site promote that interaction?
- How many sales do you expect to make each month? What additions would you like to add once you get going?
- Do the monthly profits justify the monthly costs?

Setting up a professional Web presence can be a big project and setting up an e-commerce system on top of that can be yet another big project. Be sure to consult with professionals in this field who have experience in e-commerce not just Web design.

Registering Your Domain Name

Each Web site has its own unique name, such as Amazon.com or eBay.com. This is your "domain name." It is a unique name that identifies you to all of the other computers on the Internet. There are a number of companies, known as "registrars," that will assist you in registering your Web site's name, including Network Solutions, Biz Help 101 and Dotster.

Find an easy-to-remember ".com" name for your site. Once you've successfully registered your domain name, it will remain in your name and control for as long as you pay to keep it. People who type www.yourcompanyname.com into their browsers will be taken directly to your Web site. To completely secure a name, it's not a bad idea to also buy the .net and .org extensions for it.

Your company name, trademarks, logos and artwork used on your site will require appropriate trademark and copyright protection under intellectual property laws. Your lawyer should be consulted on this issue in order to avoid unpleasant surprises (for example, the possibility of being advised that your company slogan belongs to someone else.)

Hosting your Web site

Your online business will need a place to reside. You may choose to buy (by having your own network server) or lease (by having your site hosted by a Web-hosting service). In most cases, people find it much easier to lease hosting space. For example at Biz Help 101, we lease our hosting. For a monthly fee the Web host handles the technical details, and you are free to spend your time developing content for your Web site.

Hosting services can also provide "user statistics," which track the number of visitors to your site.

Building your Web site

You will need to decide whether to hire a professional Web developer to create your Web site or to produce your own site "in-house." Both choices come with costs and benefits. If you decide to create your Web site, it is advisable to have an employee who is skilled and experienced with Web design.

If you have a real desire to learn how to create your own site, spend some time with online tutorials on creating your own site. Your credibility is at stake, and if your site is difficult to navigate, has broken links or images or out-of-date content, you will not engender trust with your customers.

Tools such as Adobe Dreamweaver® and Adobe Photoshop® allow you to create Web site without any (or much) prior knowledge of Web design. These "what you see is what you get" editors are similar to programs such as Microsoft Word in that you insert text and graphics onto your page and specify the appropriate links. Pre-defined templates give a consistent look and feel to your entire site and built-in tools allow you to globally change navigational links throughout your site.

These programs have improved significantly in recent years, but are not a perfect substitute for a professional Web developer. Advanced features are difficult to implement.

E-commerce Overview

What is e-commerce?

E-Commerce is the sale of products and services over the Internet. It is the fastest growing segment of our economy. It allows even the smallest business to reach a global audience with its product or message with minimal cost. The sale of products or services on your Web site can generate sales that will make the difference between success and failure. Even Wal-Mart, the largest retailer in the world with one billion dollars sales per day, could not anticipate the increasing wave of Internet business.

- 180 million people in the US use the Internet at least once per month.
- In 2005 there were approximately 1.08 billion people worldwide who used the internet at least once a month. This grew to 1.6 billion in 2010.
- The online population has hit 73% of all U.S. adults.
- The average income of Internet households is over $72,744, making the Internet user a very attractive customer for you to target

Is an e-commerce Web site right for your business?

Probably. Much depends on the nature of your business. Web site such as Amazon.com and Barnes & Noble have established their hold over the book market, and their sheer size, name recognition and the relationship of trust they have with their customers allows them to dominate this market with good pricing (due to economies of scale) and remarkable customer loyalty.

However, if you own a local bookstore, there are several ways to reach new customers, get them to know you better and have them keep coming back for more. You might want to offer notices of special promotions or readings by authors. Trust will become the cornerstone of building your e-business. As Warren Buffett has said, "If you don't know jewelry, know your jeweler."

A Web site doesn't need to exist solely to sell your product online. It could supplement the sales of your already established retail store. If you sell a unique product, such as wheat grass or gourmet chocolates, you might find success reaching others around the country (or the world, for that matter) who do not have access to these products in their own towns.

Using the Internet for conducting e-commerce will not assure you of being able to compete favorably with large established competitors. They already have the inventory, delivery and marketing systems in place, and they can deliver the groceries as cheap (or more cheaply) than you can. Yet, the beauty of the Internet is that it provides a global audience of potential customers and it never closes.

Your customers will have access to information about your business 24 hours a day 365 days a year. You can add pictures, audio, video, news, and so much more. Your customer will even be able to buy from you 24 hours a day. So, your Web site address should be promoted everywhere including your stationery, sales forms and advertisements.

A website can transform a local business into one engaged in global commerce. But you will need to be aware of the advantages and disadvantages of international trade outlined in our session 11 in the Building My Own Business course.

Money Transactions

There are many ways to complete money transactions online. If you already have an established Web site that your clients know you will probably want to keep it and add an e-commerce solution into it. If you do not have an e-commerce Web site you may consider e-commerce solutions offered by major online sites such as Yahoo, Amazon, and Google with little to no Web design experience needed. (Enter "commerce solutions" in the search box.) Online auction sites such as eBay, Yahoo, Google and MSN might also offer additional avenues for your business. Consider hiring and or consulting with an experienced Web designer or firm to set this up for you. Their experience can often save you time, money, and unnecessary aggravation.

Setting it all up

E-Commerce software often requires setting up a merchant account as well as establishing a payment gateway provider. A merchant account is a specialized bank account set up by a bank that allows you to accept credit cards. A payment gateway charges your customers' credit cards via the Internet and sends the funds to your merchant account. The payment gateway acts as the bridge between the merchant's Web site and the financial institutions that process transactions. Payment data is collected online from the shopper and submitted to the gateway for real-time authorization.

Several companies such as 2CheckOut.com, Authorize.Net, Cybersource.com, BizHelp101.com and Verisign.com offer various credit card transaction packages. A great start would be to try your local bank. Many banks now partner with e-commerce payment gateway solutions and can help you in most cases.

E-Commerce Considerations

- Per Cyber Source Corporation, online fraudsters took $3 billion out of e-commerce in 2006. Most companies provide at least basic forms of fraud protection.
- Be sure to take into account all your costs such as monthly e-commerce fees, packaging costs, shipping costs, time, etc.
- For internet-based orders and shipping you should check with your state's board of equalization office to determine the appropriate sales tax. Our Small Business Tax Center provides valuable links to tax information from the IRS.

Alternative methods of online payments:

Cash payments are less advanced but easier to set up. Funds are transferred from the buyer's bank account or credit card to the seller's account. This is similar to writing someone a check but much more secure and easier to track.

Below is a list of some of the more popular and well-known forms of "payment processor" systems.

- PayPal - Owned by EBay
- Google Wallet
- Biz Help 101 also has an online solution

Money transactions summary

Consider issues such as taxes, security, cost, and reliability. If your site becomes very popular, your e-commerce system will need to be scalable to that growth. Many more electronic payment companies can be found on the popular search engine Google.

Tips for Developing a Successful Site

Make your site easy to use: While it might be tempting to have a cutting-edge Web site - don't forget the basics. You will fail if a visitor can't navigate successfully through your site. Provide clear, easy-to-understand navigational tools on each page of your site. Make it easy for a visitor to find your contact information on every page.

Provide useful content: Don't just sell! These days, it's not enough to have a Web site that lists your products and provides a shopping cart for purchases. If you want your visitors to return, you'll want to provide meaningful content. A CPA's site could publish tax tips and offer links to IRS forms. A catering service could offer articles on how to host a successful party.

Encourage customer feedback via online forms and e-mail: Pay attention to the valuable information your customers can give you. Consider using online surveys such as www.zoomerang.com. Ways to improve online feedback are spelled out in our session 3 in the Building My On Business course.

Develop a mailing list: Most consumers resent junk e-mail, also called "spam." A far more appealing strategy is to develop a mailing list. Invite your customers to "opt in" to receive a newsletter or notices of specials running at your business. Make this information relevant and useful for your customer. Consider providing a "coupon" that will give them a discount on their next purchase. And, always give the recipient an easy means to "opt out" of receiving future e-mails.

Online Marketing and Promotion

There are thousands of well-designed Web sites, but very few are visible on the search engines. Almost 90 percent of Internet users today use search engines to find the information they need. Yet, many businesses are not registered with search engines. Four billion searches are done in the U.S. each month. Search engines have a great capacity to drive traffic to your site, yet few new entrepreneurs have the know-how to tap into this resource. Top search engines such as Google and Yahoo! now provide local search. Local search makes it even more important that you market your Web site effectively.

Search engines: your primary marketing tool
In the past, the methods that search engines used to rank pages were primitive and easily deciphered for savvy Webmasters to manipulate.

Times have changed and gaining a high rank on the top search engines has become extremely competitive. Today, submitting your Web site to a large number of free search engines will only result in your e-mail address being added to a large number of spam lists. Search engines are now looking to provide quality listings for their users, but also to turn a profit: hence "paid listings."

How does your Web site rank?
It is important to monitor your search engine rankings so that you can track changes, monitor the ones that you need to improve and identify engines with whom you are not listed. If your customers did a search for specific keywords on a search engine, would they find your site? Are you in the first 10 results or the first 30? The average visitor scrolls through 1.8 page results during a typical search. If your business does not appear in those first 1.8 results, that could translate to lost business.

What are people searching for?
"Search volume" is the number of times a specific keyword is searched over a period of time. Having knowledge of search volumes will give you a sense for what is being searched for and what keywords you may want to focus on. A good place to look up search volumes is through Wordtracker.com and its search suggestion tool. The goal is to find keywords or keyword phrases that you feel would drive qualified traffic to your site. Keep in mind the amount of competition for each keyword and be creative in finding different keyword combinations that others may not have tried yet.

How to manage search engine placement
It takes hard work, market research, educated decisions, and even trial and error. There are ways to improve your rankings - and actions to avoid that will hurt your rankings. While you have the option of hiring a search engine consultant to manage this important responsibility, you can also do this yourself. Here are the

factors that go into search engine placement and how to better optimize your pages for search engines.

Local Search

With the advent of "Local Search" the playing field has just gotten a whole lot more competitive. Now it is almost essential that you have an Internet presence or you will lose out to your nearest local competitor that does. Do a search on any of the major search engines and look for a "Local" tab to see how this works. Expect "Local Search" to greatly expand and improve over the years ahead.

Key components to successful search engine marketing for a Web site

- *Start with a descriptive domain name:* The domain name you choose is important. It is so very important because the name itself can help your Web site be more relevant to search engines. Pick a domain name that is easy for your clients to remember.
- *Submit to the top engines:* Submit your Web site for review and indexing only to the top search engines where people are actually doing their searches such as Google, Yahoo, MSN, etc. Be careful to read the submission guidelines for each search engine before submitting. For example, have a look at Google's search engine guidelines.
- *Focus on your homepage:* Your homepage is the single most important page on your site. Your homepage represents your business and its image. Make sure you focus on developing the content and the relevancy to search engines for this page.
- *Develop content rich pages:* Add content that includes keywords and phrases you are targeting. Many search engines consider the location of the keywords in your site along with their frequency to assess how relevant your site is to those keywords.
- *Keep an eye on your competition:* Stay informed of your competition's rankings. Top-ranked pages rank well for a reason - so see what you can do to be more competitive! Can you offer something they do not offer?
- *Add new content:* Keep your Web site fresh and updated with new content. Your visitors will appreciate it, and the search engines will look favorably upon it.
- *Networking with others:* Expand your "link popularity" by gaining more inbound links to your site. Get the word out and let other sites know about your site and how to link to it. The more links coming into your site, the more doorways you open for visitors to find you.
- *Title Tags:* Make sure the title tags across all the pages on your site are relevant to that particular page. Your domain name is not a good idea for a title tag.
- *Pay Per Click Advertising:* Consider "pay per click" strategies such as Google.com and MSN.com to enhance your overall marketing strategy.

Pay per click now offers local search options to better reach a targeted audience.

- *Review your activity logs:* "Activity logs" or "server statistics" provide you with statistics on the number of visitors coming into your site, where the visitors come from and what keywords are used. Some Web servers/hosts provide this information free. Google also offers this as a new free service called Google Analytics.
- *Checking on who links to you:* Google offers a service to determine who is linking to your Web site. Go to Google.com and in the search box type in "site:http://www.yourwebsite.com/". You can also go to bing.com: enter "site:www.yourwebsite.com/". For a complete list of Bing query language syntax, see msdn.microsoft.com

Search Engine Resources

- 1seoExperts.com

Outsourcing search engine optimization

If you would like to out source search engine optimization, ask your professional consultant for the names of previous clients or "case studies". Speak with these clients to determine what, if any, improvements they experienced. Make sure that unethical or questionable practices are not used that will be harmful in the long run.

Targeted e-mail

E-mail allows you to communicate directly with your customers. It is also one of the most abused forms of online advertising. Nobody enjoys receiving unsolicited e-mail touting a business or service. While it is possible to purchase huge mailing lists of e-mail addresses that can be used for marketing your product, you are likely to turn off large numbers of potential customers by engaging in this practice.

Instead, opt-in mailing lists are now the preferred method of establishing e-mail lists of customers who are genuinely interested in your product or service. Consider creating an online newsletter. Make it informative, useful and worth reading.

Finally, remember that each e-mail should also contain instructions for how the recipient can be removed from the e-mail list.

eBay

Whether you are starting your own business, promoting your product online, or just cleaning out your attic, eBay is definitely something you should consider. For more information, visit www.ebay.com.

How to get started
To sell on eBay, you will need to register and then verify your identity. Registration is a quick and easy process. Verification will be a little more involved, but is a necessary process to ensure that eBay remains a safe marketplace. Once you have completed these two steps, you will have a "Seller's Account" and will be able to start listing your items for sale.

Listing basics

- Decide which selling format best meets your needs. You may wish to add a Buy It Now price or Reserve price .
- Choose the optional listing upgrades you feel will help your item stand out from the rest.
- Write a good title and description. This is essential.
- Specify what payment methods you will accept, and your return policy.

Fees
When you list your item on eBay, you will pay an Insertion Fee. This fee is based on your starting price (or your reserve price if you set one). When your auction has ended, if your item sells, you will be charged a Final Value Fee based on the ending price.

Don'ts of eBay
Before you start using eBay, you need to read through their policies. Violations can cause your listings to be canceled and your account to be suspended. There are also many items that cannot be sold on eBay. Examples are firearms, drugs, fireworks, recalled items and surveillance equipment.

Get the most from your eBay experience
Supplement your commerce by providing information about your business, your products, and your policies, but most importantly a link to your Web site. This will let potential customers know where they can go to find more.

Website Top Ten Do's and Don'ts

THE TOP TEN DO'S

1. Create a Web site to compliment your business.
2. Hire a professional to create your Web site.
3. Use a .com Web site domain name that is descriptive of your business and easy to remember.
4. Register your domain name. Keep your account information in a safe place.
5. Develop a mailing list to better connect with your visitors.
6. Provide updated useful content on your Web site in order to encourage visitors to return.
7. Encourage customer feedback via online forms and e-mail.
8. Learn how to, and continually implement, ways to improve your placements on top search engines.
9. Keep your eye on your competition's rankings and get pointers from its sites.
10. Consider eBay as a means of selling your product and gaining traffic to your online store.

THE TOP TEN DON'TS

1. Assume a Web site will assure you of competing favorably with large, established competitors.
2. Turn your customers off with an unprofessional Web site.
3. Incorporate unusual or unique Web design styles that are difficult to print or save.
4. Make it difficult to navigate your site.
5. Permit out-of-date content to remain on your site.
6. Rely on graphical buttons.
7. Try to create a Web site on your own unless you are a Web designer.
8. Make it difficult for people to find your contact information.
9. Turn off your customers with unsolicited e-mail advertising.
10. Weigh your pages down with too much graphics and media.

Create a Business Plan

In our experience, the process of **creating and writing a business plan** is as valuable as the end product itself - a document that will provide the priorities, context and sanity you'll need as you start up your business.

Just remember that the most important audience for a business plan is YOU! You'll be forced to be accountable to all of the statements, claims, stats and facts inside of it.

You may also use your business plan as a tool to generate interest from financiers, prospective employees and strategic partners.

We focus on 3 aspects of business planning to consider as you write a business plan:

1. The "Defining Dozen" questions you must answer
2. Key components of a business plan
3. Writing a business plan

The "Defining Dozen" questions

To write a good business plan, you have to know the answers to the "Defining Dozen" questions. Jot down the answers to each of these questions and hang on to them. You might not use every answer in writing your business plan, but they could be helpful when you update your plan as your new business grows.

1. What's your business idea?
2. How does your idea address a need?
3. What model suits you best?
4. What's so different about what you offer?
5. How big is the market and how big will you grow?
6. What's your role going to be?
7. Who's on your team?
8. How will customers buy from you, and how much will they pay?
9. How much money do you need, and how much will you make?
10. Where's the startup money coming from?
11. How will you measure success?
12. What are your key milestones?

Once you've answered these questions, you should be prepared to write the actual business plan document.

Key components of a business plan:

Executive Summary:

Summarizes the most important information within the pages of your business plan - the people, the idea, the market, the competition, the strategy - typically no more than two pages long, the executive summary is usually written last. It takes discipline to keep the summary short, but it's a must.

Business Description:

Details the mission, goals, value proposition, business model, and key assets. After someone reads this section of the plan, they should be able to "get" what you're offering with total clarity!

Market Analysis:

Dives into the needs and wants of potential customers in the market, as well as your competition and the percentage of the market you expect to reach. Be sure to include any pertinent market research and competitive analysis you've done - and cite your sources.

Resource

To generate market size and demographic statistics for your business plan, tap into the U.S. Census or the U.S. Securities and Exchange Commission.

Marketing and Distribution:

Discusses your strategy and timeline for achieving your marketing goals and defines how you get what you offer into customers' hands. Be sure to include any new or novel ideas you have for marketing and distributing your product.

Personnel:

Describes the management team (existing or future) and any other key personnel that will be instrumental to the business' success. Includes each team member's role and responsibilities, as well as any background information that illustrates why they are highly qualified for their role.

Exit Strategy:

Puts into words what you see as the ultimate destiny of the company, especially as it may affect those who finance your new business, as well as other equity holders in the startup.

Financials:

Tool

<u>Cash Management Report</u> (419K)

Best used with Microsoft Excel 2003. Other software or versions may experience problems.

Distills your strategies and assumptions into how much they'll cost and how much money they'll make you in the course of your new business.

The Financials section should map out your first few years of business and contain:

- Written narrative of key business assumptions
- Income statement
- Balance sheet
- Statement of cash flow
- Cash management report

We've developed an important tool to help you forecast and manage the financial side of your startup business - a **cash management report**. It looks at **how cash moves in and out of your business on a monthly basis**. By preparing a cash management report before the launch of your business, you'll be able to determine if you'll need to raise outside capital, when you'll need it, and how much will be required.

Writing your Business Plan

Your business plan should be **concise and neatly formatted**. We suggest a Microsoft Word document for the bulk of the business plan, with financial documents as attached or embedded spreadsheets created in Microsoft Excel. **Avoid** fancy graphics, flowery language or photos. The easier you make it to read for a potential investor or partner, the better.

If you are the type of person who works better with templates and wizards, there are many business planning software packages available that cost around $100, as well as a few free online business plan templates.

The advantage to using business planning software is that it offers a step-by-step approach to the process (similar to a "wizard"), and can include **sample business plans** for specific types of businesses (e.g. restaurants, manufacturing, service) to help you outline some of the unique requirements or expenses associated with that particular business. It also formats your business plan for you.

A drawback to using business planning software is that it might not provide you the flexibility to convey some of the uniqueness and creativity of your new business, since it's written through the software system.

Create Key Business Assets

It's a well-known fact in the business world: Your company assets are only as good as your ability to protect them. This is especially true where intellectual property is concerned. Whether it's your company name, logo, latest invention or best-selling product, it's imperative that you take certain steps to secure your ownership rights.

We will explore seven types of key assets in this step:

1. Website Address
2. Trademarks
3. Copyrights
4. Patents
5. Provisional Applications for Patents
6. Inventor's Logs
7. Confidentiality Agreements

Types of Key Assets

Website Address (domain name)

More than ever, businesses are turning to the web for both retail opportunities and online marketing. Key to establishing a website presence is securing a website domain name for your business. (An example of a domain name is **BizHelp101.com**)

There are a number of low-cost web services that will not only register your domain name, but also set up email and websites for you, complete with e-commerce capabilities.

If you have a unique name for your company or product, be sure to immediately register it. If you discover someone else has already claimed the name you want, don't be discouraged. Often entrepreneurs allow their domain name registration to expire or are willing to sell their name to you at a reasonable price. Most domain name registration services provide contact information for domain name owners or offer a way to bid on domain names that are up for sale.

Resource

Check for your domain name availability at Network Solutions, GoDaddy.com, BizHelp101.net or Register.com.

Trademarks

A trademark is one of the most important business assets you'll ever own. It's your brand name, your logo, or any other symbol that distinguishes your company or your company's goods from those of another manufacturer. By registering your trademark you go on record as the official owner of the mark, which gives you a significant leg up in court should a dispute over your right to use the mark ever arise. This comes in handy, for example, if you discover that another person or company is hurting your business reputation or causing confusion by using your mark to sell similar or cheaper-quality goods.

An owner of an unregistered mark may indicate ownership of a mark with the symbol "TM" for a trademark, or "SM" for a service mark.

In general, generic marks do not receive trademark protection because they are so general. On the other hand, owners of a registered mark are entitled to use the registration symbol ® in connection with their mark.

Resource

BizHelp101.com has a comprehensive screening tool that saves you time and legal fees by identifying terms and logos that are already trademarked.

You can earn more about how to file a trademark at the U.S. Patents and Trademarks website.

Copyrights

It's not uncommon for people to confuse copyrights with trademarks. Whereas trademarks are used to protect intellectual property such as company names, brands, logos and symbols, a copyright grants you exclusive legal rights to your creative work, which can include anything from literary or website content to musical or artistic compositions. In order to receive copyright protection for your work, your creation must be expressed in a tangible form such as a piece of writing or a recording. Once granted, a copyright prevents others from copying, performing or using your work without your permission.

Resource

Learn more about how to file a copyright.

Patents

If you have a bright idea, don't wait for someone else to turn it into a commercial success. You should quickly protect your invention (assuming it is novel) so you can cash in first. The best way to protect your idea is to get a patent on it. A patent is a property right granted by the Government to an inventor "to exclude others from making, using, offering for sale, or selling the invention throughout the United States or importing the invention into the United States" for a limited time in exchange for public disclosure of the invention when the patent is granted. There are three kinds of patents, including: utility patents, design patents, and plant patents.

1. Utility patents may be granted to anyone who invents a useful process, a machine, an article of manufacture, or a composition of matter.
2. Design patents may be granted to anyone who invents a new, original, and ornamental design for an article of manufacture.
3. Plant patents may be granted to anyone who invents or discovers and asexually reproduces any distinct and new variety of plants.

A common misconception is that the patent gives its owner the right to make, use, or sell the invention. The patent only gives the owner the ability to *exclude others* from making, using or selling the invention. In a standard scenario, patents last for twenty years. The twenty years begins on the date that an application for a non-provisional or provisional patent was first filed. In deciding to patent your invention, we always recommend consulting a patent attorney.

Provisional Applications for Patents

A Provisional Application is a fast and easy way to temporarily protect your invention until you're ready to commit the time and money required to submit a full patent application. Think of it as a legal placeholder.

Because the application to secure patents is a lengthy and expensive process, the USPTO created a provisional patent which allows you to temporarily protect your invention. The non-provisional application establishes the filing date of your patent application and begins the examination process. A provisional application only establishes your filing date and expires automatically after one year.

You may file a provisional application if you are not ready to enter your application into the regular examination process. A provisional application establishes a filing date at a lower cost for a first patent application filing in the United States.

A Provisional Application makes sure no one else rushes in and claims your invention while you're busy fine-tuning your design, securing funds, or testing your idea's market potential. A provisional application allows the term "Patent Pending" to be applied to your invention which can be useful in warding off any imitators.

But be careful. Provisional patents can come back to bite you later. You might find yourself limited or locked-in to what you describe in it, even though you've come up with additional improvements during your year-long provisional period.

If you go this route, we highly recommend that you at least include legitimate "claims," a key part of a formal patent. Otherwise, you should contact an attorney to patent your invention, or at least help you complete the application .

Resource

Learn more about how to file a Provisional Application.

Inventor's Logs

The United States Patent and Trademark Office awards a patent to the first person who can prove they've invented a new product. An Inventor's Log Book helps you establish that you were the first to develop your idea by recording the progress of your inventing. You should begin using an inventor's log the moment you conceive of an idea and continue to keep a detailed record of your activities as you develop your idea into reality.

Creating an Inventor's Log

In order to prove that you are the inventor of a specific invention, you should document and memorialize all information in an "inventor's log". U.S. Patent requires that you are the inventor of any invention claimed in a patent application and keeping an inventor's log may prove invaluable should you ever need to substantiate inventorship. A patent log also can be valuable if you need to prove that you were the first to invent a particular invention.

The inventor's log is literally a diary. The first entry should be posted when you conceive of your idea. This first entry should describe the invention, how you came upon it, the place, the circumstances, and any preliminary conceptual details. As you develop your invention, include in your inventor's log all engineering and testing data, drawings, research data, as well as any information related to similar products or patents you discover. It's also important to record the names of anybody to whom you disclose your idea and the details relating to any such disclosures or meetings.

Your log entries should be kept in chronological order with entries posted one after the other on consecutively numbered pages, written in pen, and dated. Entries can take the form of strictly text, or could be drawings, or both. If you finish an entry partway down a page, do not start the next entry on the next page, rather post entries one right after the other in contiguous order. It is also beneficial to have an unbiased witness sign and date an entry if such a witness is conveniently available. It's important that you select a logbook with pages that cannot be added or subtracted without it being evident.

Should anyone else participate in the development of the invention, it's very important that you detail the contribution and clarify whether or not this participation resulted in an activity of inventor ship or not. In order for a patent to be valid, all inventors must be named on the application.

Keep your notebook or notebooks in a secure location, and regularly photocopy or scan entries to keep a complete second copy of the log should the original get damaged or lost. Keep the copy in a separate location.

Confidentiality Agreements

Anytime you are considering exposing some of your company's secrets, whether it is a customer list, business process or financial data that you want to keep out of the hands of the competition, it is critical that you safeguard this information. With a Confidentiality Agreement, also called a Non-Disclosure Agreement or NDA, you can do just that. Typically, there are two types of NDAs: "One-Way" and "Mutual." When you hire a new employee or offer information to a potential business partner, a one-way NDA provides the protection you need in case the potential employee or business partner decides not to come onboard or engage you in business. When information is being passed both ways, each party should sign a mutual NDA.

Find the Funding

This is a critical step. You've got to find funding for your business but ensure that it's the right *kind* of funding. Yes, there's the adage, "beggars can't be choosers," but the fact is, you must be selective and smart when seeking money for your startup or it could turn your dream business into a nightmare.

To identify which form of financing is just right for you, think about your long-term personal and business goals and the type of business you're planning to launch.

Money comes in many forms, from tapping credit cards and taking equity out of your home to government grants and high net worth "angel" financing.

We will tackle seven ways to fund your business in this step:

1. Bootstrapping

2. Debt Financing

3. Grants

4. Friends and Family

5. Angel Investors

6. Factoring

7. Venture Capitalists

8. Corporations

Ways to Fund your Business

95% businesses need funding and the following are some of the ways you can get the funding for your new business and Idea.

Bootstrapping

Look no further than yourself to find the funding you need—perhaps using your savings, your initial revenues, credit cards, equity pulled from your home, etc.

Upside

- You maintain complete financial and operational control over your business.
- No equity-holders to pay off if the company hits it big.
- If you are able to use savings, you won't have monthly payments to add to your business' expenses.

Downside

- If the business fails, you may face a lot of personal debt.
- Depending on the source of your personal capital, you may end up paying a high interest rate (if you use a credit card), or you may miss out on earning interest (if you use savings).
- Typically, this form of funding limits the amount of money you have for strategic purposes and the rate of growth of your business can be significantly slowed down as it starves for cash.

Debt Financing

Debt financing requires that you qualify for a traditional bank loan (not common for raw startups), or that you find a bank that can provide you a loan with a SBA guaranty.

Before you land a loan, you need to understand how to maximize your odds for success in landing a loan. The lending process is inherently a tough one, but it's also a system that has been the catalyst of success for many small businesses. In fact, some entrepreneurs would say that their relationship with their banker has been the pivotal ingredient to growth.

Upside

- You don't have to give up equity, proceeds or control in order to get funded.
- You build a powerful relationship with your banker that can open up additional forms of debt financing you may need down the road.

Downside

- Bank loans typically go to existing small businesses with 2 years of history and credit.
- You must pay interest, and if you don't keep up with your loan payments, you could find yourself in a tough spot with the bank.
- You may be required to provide personal collateral, such as your home, to obtain the loan.

Grants

Grants are special programs designed to fuel the innovative fires of small businesses, and typically target specific groups or types of businesses, such as technology businesses, veteran-owned businesses, women-owned businesses and minority-owned businesses.

Upside

- You don't pay interest – grants are essentially "free money."
- Potential investors (should you be seeking additional funding) love the "leverage" that grants provide.

Downside

- The competition is stiff for grants, and grant writing (applying for the grants) is an art form, so you may want to find a grant writer to help you.
- How you can use grant funds is strictly defined by the organization that provides them.

Resource

- Grant resources
- Find other government grants through each specific department
- Find specific grants dealing with the development of technology

Friends and Family

Just like it sounds, raise money from people you know well, either in exchange for equity or as a loan to be repaid.

Upside

- This option has the fewest contractual strings attached, although you should still draw up a contract to protect your friend's or family member's investment.
- Funds are typically available quickly.

Downside

- This is usually a limited, one-time source of funding.
- You are spending your friend's or family member's money – so do so wisely, and be prepared to deal with the consequences if your business does not succeed.

Resource

To better manage loans between friends and family, Circle lending provides a full range of services for managing financial transactions between private parties.

Angel Investors

Angel investors are individuals who invest in companies at an early stage in exchange for equity and the chance to help guide the company. In contrast, venture capitalists invest as a profession and generally on behalf of other investors.

Generally one is ready to approach angels when they have exhausted their friends and family but are not yet ready to approach venture capitalists for money.

Approach angels if you are looking for large amounts ($25K to $1M) of "smart money"—the people who provide this form of funding have already "made it big" in their own careers and can help guide you to do the same.

Upside

- Angels invest more than money - they provide mentoring and contacts.
- Angels are patient about their investment.
- There are no monthly payments with this type of financing – angels make their money when you achieve your business' exit strategy.

Downside

- Angels are difficult to find.
- Angels deserve regular and thorough reporting, which can take up valuable time.
- You are giving up equity in your company.

Resource

Here's a directory of angel investor networks and organizations that link entrepreneurs to angel investors.

Factoring

Factoring is where the financial institution (factor) advances the entrepreneur money against proceeds from the entrepreneur's outstanding accounts receivables. Factoring firms generally are paid a percentage of the invoice's value.

Upside

- Provides funds quickly, when they might not otherwise be available.
- Helps companies with an unsteady and unbalanced cash flow.

Downside

- Factoring requires increased accounting oversight and administration.
- A substantial "cost of money" is involved in factoring. A hefty portion of your receivables will go the way of the factoring firm.
- Your customers are actually paying a factoring company rather than you.

Venture Capitalists

Venture capitalists are individuals or companies with large amounts of capital to invest and expect higher returns.

Use Venture Capitalists if you already have a great track record in your field or as an entrepreneur, and if you have a business concept that will require a lot of money ($250K to $10s of millions) and will have a rapid growth curve.

Upside

- VCs invest smarts and networking, in addition to money.
- VCs typically have more money available if you need it to grow down the road.

Downside

- VCs typically only invest in established companies.
- You must be willing to give up significant control over major decisions for your company.
- You must have a "fast growth" company.
- You must have an aggressive exit strategy to sell your business or do an IPO within 5-7 years.

Funding through Corporations

What is a Corporation?

Although a corporation is separate and distinct from its stockholders, directors or officers, it is a separate entity that can act only through its members, officers, or agents and cannot have knowledge or belief of any subject independent of the knowledge or belief of its people. A stockholder (owner or partial owner) is a holder of shares of stock in the corporation and is NOT IN LEGAL DANGER for the acts of the corporation. In other words, you, as the owner, are not responsible. A stockholder is not the employer of those working for the corporation nor is he the owner of corporate property.

A corporation is a citizen in the state wherein it was created and does not cease to be a citizen of its state of domicile by engaging in business or acquiring property in another state. Since corporations are solely creatures of Statute, their powers are derived from the constitution and laws of the state in which it is incorporated. As an artificial person, a corporation is considered to have its domicile in the state where it is incorporated and the place where it has a statutory presence. When the corporation functions in a different state, the site of its designated resident or registered agent is sometimes called its "statutory domicile."

The existence of the corporation is not affected by the death or bankruptcy of a shareholder, officer, or director. It has a continuous existence as long as it complies with the statutory requirements of the state where it is incorporated.

For the purposes of raising capital and building credit for a small to medium sized business, corporations provide the best chances for gaining approval and are recommended. A corporation is a separate legal entity from the owners and officers of the business. It files a SS-4 form with the Internal Revenue Service to obtain a tax identification number that will be used to file taxes and can be used to create the company's own credit profile. Corporations are the oldest business entity in the United States and have the most case histories.

Credit card companies have designed credit cards just for corporations. Venture capitalists and banks will spend more time with the owners of a corporation than that of a sole proprietorship. Corporations are taken more seriously in business. Some companies will not hire another business unless it is incorporated.

There are several types of corporations, but the two that are most commonly used are the "S" and "C."

To decide which of the two is best for your situation, consult a tax professional.

C Corporations are there:

1. Own entity

    – They have their own EIN

        – What is an EIN? Employer Identification Number (EIN) is also known as a
        – Federal Tax Identification Number
        – An EIN is like a Social Security number for corporations

2. Corporations can Establish it's own credit Business credit ratings is called a "Paydex Score"

Generated by these two companies:

    • DnB (Dun & Bradstreet) or Experian business.

    • Paydex isn't a FICO score (Personal credit score) but are similar in a way that both are used to determine whether you'll get a credit and on what terms.

    • The Paydex Score ranges
        o from 0 to 100, with 90-100 as excellent scores;
        o 80 and below as good;
        o 70 and below as bad scores.
    For obvious reason, higher scores indicate better payment performance.

Corporations Start with no Credit, and the corporation must established credit. Lenders may require a personal guarantor for credit cards issued to corporations depending on the size and financial assets of the company. A personal guarantor can help the lender minimize its risk by securing a party responsible for the corporation's potential debt. Signing up as a personal guarantor, however, brings with it a large amount of liability.

The following is several ways to establish Business Credit:

Ways to establish corporate credit

1. **Your Credit-**
   If you have a FICO score of 650 or better with a corporation you can get start up money for your business. You utilize your personal credit as the Personal Guarantor: A personal guarantor gives his guarantee that he will pay a debt. For a corporate credit card, the personal guarantor signs a legally binding agreement with the card lender. In this agreement, the guarantor assumes responsibility for the credit card bills the corporation incurs in the event the corporation doesn't pay the debt.

2. **O.P.C. Other Peoples Credit-**
   Personal Guarantor: A personal guarantor can be a shareholder or owner of the company, or he can be an unaffiliated third party.

   Guarantor Default
   Once the corporation fails to pay, the credit card lender will seek payment of the bill from the guarantor. If the guarantor also defaults, the lender can seek recourse against the guarantor. The lender may decide to sue the guarantor in court. The agreement the guarantor signed gives the card lender the right to file legal action in order to recoup payment. This civil lawsuit may result in the issuance of a judgment against the guarantor.

   Consequences
   If the credit card lender receives a judgment against the guarantor, the lender can use that judgment to pursue the guarantor's assets. A judgment is a decree issued by the court that specifies the guarantor's responsibility for the debt and the amount owed. Depending on the state, a judgment owner can seize funds in the guarantor's bank accounts, place a lien on the guarantor's property or garnish a portion of the guarantor's wages in order to satisfy the debt.

   Considerations
   An individual shareholder isn't responsible for the debts of the corporation. If a shareholder agrees to be a personal guarantor, however, she loses that protection. Also, if the guarantor does pay a credit card bill on behalf of the corporation, the guarantor has a legal right of action against the corporation to recover those funds. Furthermore, although the lender will pursue the guarantor for the debt, that does not prevent the lender from pursuing the corporation if it's unable to obtain sufficient payment from the guarantor. If the corporation is insolvent, or if the guarantor is insolvent, the lender may ultimately not recoup those funds at all.

There are ways to protect the PG's assets, and we offer workshops and personal consultation.

3. **Add Business Trade lines**
   a. Business trade lines are lines of credit extended to businesses by their vendors, by which the business receives goods or services for which it agrees to pay at a later date. Businesses may have trade lines with many different vendors, and they generally agree to pay 30, 60 or 90 days after receipt of the goods and services.
   b. How Trade Lines Are Established. Trade lines are often established between a business and a vendor, as opposed to a line of credit offered by a bank. A building supplies store, for example, might order several pallets of pine lumber and agree to pay the lumber mill 30 days after receipt. This enables the business owner to sell the lumber and pay the costs of its stock out of sales revenue. A vendor may pull the company's credit report to decide if it is creditworthy before extending a trade line, and in some cases may review a small business owner's personal credit report, especially if business credit has not been established.
   c. Who Uses Trade Lines- Not all small businesses use credit. But three-fifths of small businesses that do use credit use trade credit lines, according to the U.S. Small Business Administration. Businesses that use trade credit tend to have lots of assets and liquidity, or access to cash, but many also have more debt than companies that don't use credit. Construction and manufacturing are two industries that tend to use credit.
   d. Impact on Credit Score- Using trade lines can help businesses build credit since the loans are frequent and the turnaround quick. They can also help rapidly build positive credit experiences. However, because vendors are not required to report credit experiences with a business to any reporting agency, a business could spend years creating a positive credit record that never shows up on a credit report. If possible, establish trade lines with companies that report regularly. Unlike individual credit scores, business credit scores range from 1 to 100; 75 is considered a very good score.

4. Seasoned Lines of Credit

There are many companies online promising to sell trade lines. Many of these are selling "seasoned" trade lines. If your company has poor or little credit, you can, for several hundred or several thousand dollars, have your business piggybacked onto the account of someone who has established excellent credit. This enables new business owners to appear to have more creditworthiness than they have established for themselves. While seasoned credit is legal, it can wind up costing business owners more than obtaining their own credit at higher interest rates, according to the credit reporting agency Experian. It is also an easy way for someone who isn't experienced at managing credit to get into financial trouble.

5. Self / Aged Corporations

A **shelf corporation**, **shelf company**, or **aged corporation**, is a company or corpora<on that has had no activity. It was created and let with no activity - metaphorically put on the "shelf" to "age". The company can then be sold to a person or group of persons who wish to start a company without going through all the procedures of creating a new one.

6. New Credit Profile Number called Secondary Credit Number (SCN)

What is a Secondary Credit Number (SCN)?

The CPN or SCN (Secondary Credit Number)

A secondary credit number(SCN) is a nine-digit number that has the exact same genetic makeup of a Social Security Number. It is simply an available file number at the credit bureaus that can have financial information and payments reported. You have the right to establish this number only once, so do not abuse it. This explanation is not here to advise anyone to misrepresent your Social Security Number, as you are completely responsible for any debts you incur using your Secondary Credit Number. -Wikipedia

A Secondary Credit Number can be used in place of your Social Security Number when applying for credit. All SCN numbers are privately issued numbers that do not replace your current Social Security Number. An SCN number can not be used for government purposes.
It is your legal right to keep your Social Security Number private, and use a separate number for any credit related purposes. You are only required by law to disclose your Social Security Number to the Internal Revenue Service, your employer, when registering a motor vehicle, buying a firearm, or applying and obtaining a federally-insured loan such as FHA, Sallie Mae, etc. We encourage you to use the laws to your advantage.

Note* Obtaining a secondary credit number will not release you from any previous debt you may have. You are still legally responsible for your own debt obtained through your Social Security Number. All a secondary credit number is doing for you is giving you a second chance and a new credit profile!

Yes Secondary credit numbers are LEGAL, based on the 1974 Privacy Act, as long as you don't abuse the number. You can use the existing laws to your advantage for a change. Due to certain rights guaranteed by the 1974 US Privacy Act Title V you have the right to keep your Social Security Number private and not be denied service due to your refusal. The credit bureaus are not government agencies, so you do not have to give them your Social Security Number. To answer the question, YES if used properly. Thousands of people have done it over the past 30yrs and continue to do so.
You are still responsible for the debts on your social security number .We suggest not to use the SCN as a way to avoid any debt (defraud creditors) under your Social Security Number. You are responsible for all debts on your old report and debts incurred with your Secondary credit number. You must remember that while you are rebuilding your credit, you must use your new SCN wisely. If you have had troubled credit in the past, don't repeat your mistakes.

Once a SCN number is obtained you are can add personal trade lines to the file. There are companies in business that will legally add what is called authorized users and more.

You can use any or all these ways to get the funding for your business. Depending on your budget is the way(s) you go.

Now that you have the information, what are you waiting on get up and get going! Once the Paydex and FICO scores are in place you are ready for business funding. There are programs out there where you don't need a PG just a 80+ Paydex score, but just let you know when the banking industry went upside down, their lending practices are now different. See FinanceBuilders.biz and contact our finance specialist to help you get your company set up and get funding.

Organize Logistics

Logistics are not the most exciting aspect of starting up a business, but having your logistics in order can mean the difference between success and failure. Having your books in order, your contracts buttoned up, your money safely managed and your downside covered are each critical to your personal and business future. **Accountants, lawyers, bankers, insurance agents**—the big four—are some of the people that can help you get organized and put you on a path to starting up *smart*. These service providers will be instrumental as you grow, too.

In addition to the "big four," there are other service providers that may be vital to your business success. For example, you might need a website developer or a realtor – it just depends on your business model and plan.

Before you start your search for these service providers, it's important to know what you want to accomplish with each of them, and to set a well-defined budget to meet your goals. Once you've hired these professionals, you should work with them to establish clear milestones to reach, a strict timeline for reaching them and a plan for communicating with each other along the way.

Regardless of who you retain, they should be well-versed in assisting entrepreneurs, and they should understand the nature of your industry. Most importantly, you should be able to trust them. Therefore, the best way to find these service providers is through referrals from your friends and business associates.

In this step, we will focus on nine areas of logistics:

1. Accounting
2. Legal Services
3. Insurance
4. Banking
5. Information Technology
6. Website Development
7. Merchant Banking/e-Commerce
8. Travel
9. Real Estate

1. Accounting

Accountants bring structure and order to your business and help you plan for current and future needs. They can help you choose a structure for your business, file the paperwork to do so, and advise you on tax-related issues and account management. Accountants can also help you set up financial timelines with potential revenue and expenses so that you can accurately project your company's cash flow.

Once your business is formed, accountants can assist you with ongoing bookkeeping, payroll and financial analysis and management. In fact, many businesses bring in an outside accountant once a week to assist with payroll and bookkeeping.

Like attorneys, accountants generally charge by the hour or on a project basis, depending on the work. The amount charged can vary by geographic location and experience level of the accountant.

Questions to ask a prospective accountant:

1. Do you specialize in businesses like mine?
2. Are you qualified to prepare income tax returns as well as keep my books?
3. Can you provide me with references from clients similar to me?
4. Can you explain your fee structure?
5. Are you a CPA (certified public accountant)?

You'll also need an accounting software package like Microsoft Office Accounting or Quickbooks to track all of the financial transactions in your business on a daily basis. Maintaining your financials in an accounting program helps you stay organized throughout the year, and makes things much easier come tax time when your accountant needs to decipher your books and prepare your tax returns.

2. Legal Services

Attorneys help you strategize and formalize key relationships with vendors, product sources, financiers and employees. They can also help you form your company, draft contracts and non-disclosure agreements with vendors or other parties, and comply with a sea of regulations ranging from zoning and securities to environmental and Sarbanes-Oxley. If you are an inventor, a patent attorney is particularly important for you, as they can help you conduct patent searches and file your patent paperwork.

You need to select an attorney who is an expert in the area of law with which you need help. The best way to find an attorney is to ask your friends, accountant, banker, business associates or vendors for recommendations. You can also check with your state or local bar association, or search a directory like the ones at Lawyers.com, but these sources may not have direct experience with the listed attorneys. Therefore, it is important to interview prospective attorneys carefully yourself.

Attorneys generally charge an hourly rate for research, writing and negotiation. In addition, they typically bill for things like filing fees, telephone calls, copies, and work done by other professionals within the firm. Fees depend on the experience of the attorney, the size and geographic location of the law firm, the matter being worked on and the client's financial situation. Some cases may be worked out on a project fee basis.

Questions to ask a prospective attorney:

1. Have you handled matters like mine, and can you give me examples?
2. What is your track record of working with companies of my size, stage and industry?
3. What will the timeline be for completion of this work?
4. How will you keep me informed of your progress?
5. What assurances can you give me that I will be a priority client?
6. What is a ballpark figure for the total bill, including fees and expenses?
7. Will you be working on my file, or will an associate work on the file to cut costs? (i.e. can junior attorneys or paralegals in your office handle some of the administrative work at a lower rate?)
8. Do you have sample legal forms and agreements that I can use for my business?
9. Would you be willing to work out a more creative fee structure based upon the success of my business, or perhaps accept fee for service?

Resource

To better understand how lawyers charge for their services, visit the American Bar Association.

3.   Insurance

Health insurance is a particularly hot topic these days, and it probably comes as no surprise to hear that costs are increasing exponentially each year. Health insurance costs are, in fact, one of the number one concerns of most small business owners. An economical source to consider for health insurance is your local chamber of commerce. Oftentimes, chambers group their members' companies together to obtain deep discounts on health insurance, discounts you might not otherwise have access to on your own.

You can also obtain insurance through an agent. Insurance agents make their money through commissions on the products they sell, so there should not be any upfront cost to you. You should seek out several agents, obtain quotes and go with your gut. Insurance agents can counsel you as to what kinds of insurance you will need and the type of coverage available to you, such as health insurance, property insurance, general liability insurance, workers compensation and malpractice insurance.

Questions to ask a prospective insurance agent:

1. Are you a licensed agent?
2. How many companies do you currently represent?
3. Are you independent or do you work for an insurance brokerage/agency?
4. How long has your agency been in business and how long have you been with the agency?
5. If you are independent, how many insurance carriers do you work with?
6. What kind of insurance do you sell?
7. Have you worked with businesses like mine before?
8. What types of value-added services do you provide - employee benefits, retirement planning, wealth management, human resources outsourcing?
9. Do you offer 24/7 service?
10. How do you perceive your role in handling claims?
11. How often will you review my policies to see if better prices or coverage are available?

Resource

For more information on obtaining insurance visit the National Association of Insurance Commissioners.

4. Banking

Even if you don't need or qualify for a loan yet, banks do provide a suite of other products fundamental to your business that are mostly (but not completely) financial in nature. These can include business checking accounts, business credit cards and perhaps even a credit reference from your banker. Banks also have great contacts in the community and can be an excellent source of business referrals.

It's vital for you to separate your business and personal finances early on, to simplify bookkeeping and tax returns. Open a business checking account at your local bank to start things off on the right foot.

You should also establish a relationship with your banker early on, so you can learn from him how best to position yourself for a loan down the road (if you will need one). Your banker can also keep you apprised of what other financial products might be appropriate for your particular business such as merchant banking services, payroll services, treasury management services and much more.

5. Information Technology

Information technology (IT) encompasses a lot of things, including purchasing computers, setting up computer networks, security measures, email systems, software, backing up business data, high-speed internet access, and phone systems.

The extent of the IT services you'll need depends on your business model, and you may or may not need or want to hire an IT professional to assist you. If you plan to go it alone, tap into resources like the Small Business Technology Institute or the Microsoft Small Business Center for articles and online training on a variety of IT topics.

If you decide to hire an IT consultant to help set up and support your computer system on a one-time or ongoing basis, you should ask for referrals from business associates, your trade association or the retailer from which you purchase your computer equipment.

Questions to ask a prospective IT consultant:

1. Do you specialize in my industry and in assisting small businesses?
2. What will your availability be if I have an urgent problem?
3. Do you charge a retainer or by the hour, and do you charge for any other expenses?
4. What services do you offer - website hosting, ongoing consulting and troubleshooting?

6. Website Development

Your website may be the backbone of your entire company, especially if you are an online retailer. And there are a wide variety of options for developing your website, so choose carefully. For example, there are online services, like Microsoft Office Live and Template Monster, that will provide you with the tools to create your own site using templates, and they'll even set up your web hosting for you.

If you need a customized and complex site, you may decide to hire a website designer and programmer. Designers create the look and feel of the site, and design any artwork, while programmers are the ones who build the "back-end" of your site and make it actually function. It's also possible to find a professional who is both a designer and a programmer, if you prefer to go that route.

Regardless of which path you take, you must first decide what you want in a website.

Here are a few things to consider:

1. What is the primary purpose of the site? Do you want to sell products (e-commerce)? Do you need to provide information? Will your site contain multimedia elements like music and video? All of the above?
2. Will you host the site, or do you need someone to host it?
3. How often will the site need to updated?
4. Do you want to be able to update the site yourself or pay someone else to update it?
   There are content management systems available that let non-technical staff update images, text, and pages on a website.
5. Who will develop the content for the site?

And finally, if you're operating on a tight budget that really doesn't allow for hiring a website development firm, you can ask if an individual developer is willing to do the work on a freelance basis.

Questions to ask a prospective website developer:

1. Do you have experience in designing and programming a site similar to mine?
2. Do you design and program yourself, or do you outsource some of the work?
3. What is the timeline for designing and programming my site?
4. How many designs will you "mock-up" for me to review?
5. Do you charge by the hour or by the project?
6. How many corrections am I allowed to make before you charge me for additional work?
7. Will you also host the site and secure a domain name?
8. Do you have experience building search-engine friendly websites, and can you provide examples of sites you've designed that rank well in natural search engine results?
9. Can you point me toward a sample portfolio of websites you have designed?
10. Can you provide me with your website address so that I can take a look? (You can tell a lot by looking at a web design company's site. Would you hire a plumber whose own kitchen sinks is leaking? The same holds true for website developers)

7.   Merchant Banking

If you are planning to accept credit cards as a form of payment, you must have a merchant banking account. Merchant banking accounts can be tough to come by for startup businesses.

Factors that merchant banks take into consideration:

1. Whether you already have an established business
2. The type of product(s) you are offering and the amount of sales volume you expect
3. Your credit risk, including personal credit history
4. Whether you have ever applied for bankruptcy
5. Whether you appear on the Terminated Merchant File List or MATCH file
6. Whether you have a website and clearly state your return policy
7. Whether you have ever been convicted of credit card fraud or a related felony

To find a merchant banking service, the best place to start is your current bank. If you qualify for a merchant banking account, you will need to invest in some hardware and software to process transactions. There will also be fees associated with your application, each transaction, each statement and customer support.

Resource

If you **don't qualify for a merchant banking** account just yet, and you want to operate an e-commerce business, a service such as PayPal and Square are companies that offers merchant services. They allow you accept credit cards online without a merchant account and works with many of the shopping cart systems available. They offer various solutions to help you be able to take credit and debit cards for sales transactions.

Both services offer free tools such as a card reader that works with smartphones and tablets. There are not upfront costs for the resources you pay per transaction.

8.   Travel

If you're starting a business that will have you or your staff traveling frequently to trade shows and client meetings, it's a good idea to leverage the Internet for discounted travel options. Additionally, setting up frequent traveler reward accounts with your preferred airline, hotel and car rental company will help you accrue points towards free tickets, hotel stays, and maybe even upgrades and amenities.

Going the traditional route of using a travel agent is certainly still an option, and could be the right one if you frequently have complex itineraries and no time to shop for good prices yourself. Searching websites that aggregate discounted prices from a variety of airlines, hotels and car rental companies is also a simple way to get a broad sampling of your options. But some airlines and hotels offer better deals directly at their own websites, and may not even participate in the aggregated travel sites, so be sure to shop around.

9.   Real Estate

If you are opening a brick-and-mortar store or an office, you will, of course, need some real estate. You can choose to lease a property or buy one, but in either case, it's best to begin with the Downtown Development Authority or the City's Planning Commission in the community in which you want to locate. These entities may be able to help you identify the perfect location for your business, perhaps even one that carries some attractive tax incentives. Otherwise, you may try working with a commercial real estate agent or developer to identify the right location. A real estate agent or broker will take a commission on the sale price or lease, just as they do in personal real estate transactions.

To find a commercial real estate agent near you, ask for references from other small business owners in your community, or peruse the online directories.

Questions to ask a prospective realtor:

1. Do you have many properties listed in my desired region?
2. How often will you contact me about available listings?
3. Do you have a website where I can view properties online?
4. Do you represent both the buyer and the seller?
5. What commission level do you charge?

Resources

- If you just need a place to hold meetings, or a workstation for a few weeks or months to get your business off the ground, companies like Regus offers what is called Executive Office Suites: professional offices, meeting rooms and virtual offices.

- Today, there are what is called Co-Working Spaces. Works the almost the same as Executive Office Suites. The main differences is that there are more support from the small businesses and there is some training also offered.

- "Incubators" is another system that has resurged on steroids. Mainly for those that have an invention, right now mainly found in places like San Francisco, New York's Soho, they offer a solution that is fantastic; You become a part of an eco-system that the owner offers almost everything needed to develop a product (Widget). They offer from drafting tables, computers, prototype 3d printers and more.

These are powerful ways to get the support needed to help you get your business started.

Find Great People

In a small business, the impact of a single team member can be enormous. Every person you add to your team must be a star. Is that possible? Absolutely. First, make sure you define what a star is within each role of your company. Then you can go find them.

We'll focus on four action items in this step:

1. Understanding the Power of People
2. Find the stars to bring onto your team
3. Keep your stars
4. Importance of a mentor

The Power of People

The single most important factor in the success of a company is its people. It all starts with you as the entrepreneur and flows from there to everyone on your team. Great people can take a mediocre idea and turn it into success. But no matter how great the idea is, if you have mediocre people on the team it will not succeed. We have asked many angel investors and venture capitalists what the most important factor is in determining whether they will invest in a company. It's the quality of the people. Successful entrepreneurs say the same thing. It's star people that have made their businesses shine.

In tapping into the power of people, you must understand that it is the personal relationships that you have or can cultivate that will make the difference in your ability to attract stars to your team. If you are proactive about building those relationships, you will have a much greater opportunity for success. The challenge is that it's not easy to invest your personal energy and time. It seems like a slow process. The reality is that you are at a great advantage as a small business. You can utilize your personality and uniqueness in a way that larger businesses cannot. Take advantage of that.

Finding Your Superstars

You must be proactive if you are going to attract superstars to your team. A college football coach goes after coveted high school seniors by sitting at the kitchen table with the recruit and mom and dad. You can hire people by placing ads but you run the risk of attracting walk-ons. Superstars need to be pursued. Here is a proactive strategy to increase your odds of adding stars to your team:

Create a superstar list. Write down the names of 12 people that you would like to work with. Don't limit the list to people who could fit a current need on your team. Just choose stars, no matter what their specific gifts are.

Now here's the key step ... CALL THEM!! Tell each of the 12 that you have selected them to be on this elite superstar list and the reasons why. They will be appropriately flattered and motivated to want to help you build your team of stars. They may personally be in a season of their lives where they will join you. But even they are not, they will be able to point you to other stars to pursue. Stars know how to identify other stars.

Bonus Strategy

If you already have a team that you are building upon, ask each of your team members to create their own superstar list of 12. Encourage them to proactively reach out to those stars even when you are not in an official "hiring" mode. Developing relationships in advance of the moment of need is extremely productive. Create a budget of both time and dollars so that you and your employees can cultivate superstar relationships. Remember, superstars need to be pursued.

Look for three types of people for your superstar list:

1. People with **potential**
2. People with **proven skills**
3. People who are what we call **"power brokers"**

Hiring people with potential allows for growth into a position and keeps the employee motivated over a longer period of time (this works even at executive levels in your company). It's also less expensive. Hiring people with proven skills will allow you to quickly fill in areas where your team is weak. Power brokers have both skills and can wield influence in your community or industry.

Posting on Job Boards

If you want an influx of resumes to make your selections from you can consider posting your open position on internet job boards. Your company will get worldwide or regional exposure depending on what sites you choose. This can be helpful for you to gain an understanding of the average candidate that is currently actively hunting for a new job. You can use this information to compare to the stars that you are cultivating through your proactive strategy.

It's even possible that you will find a diamond in the rough. But realize that you will need to budget a good deal of time and energy to sift through all of the responses and you have an obligation to respond to every person who submits a resume.

Resource

Many of the large job boards have automated this process to make it as efficient as possible: Post your open position on a national job board like Monster, CareerBuilder, or HotJobs.

Keep Your Superstars

Remember the great advantage that small businesses have. You're small! You can be more personalized. Create an environment that is unique, flexible and customized. You can! Bigger companies can't.

Three Strategies to Retain your Stars

Customized perks

Ask your team what they want. Instead of traditional cash-oriented perks, some may prefer a gym membership, others a flexible work schedule. Customization is a great way to compete against bigger companies who can offer your employees bigger salaries and better benefits.

Recognize the whole team

People are attracted to small companies because they like being a part of an intimate team. Be careful about singling out only a few people on a regular or long-term basis. This can be more hurtful than beneficial to a small team's chemistry.

Communicate more than you think is necessary

Special events like monthly barbecues and field trips to ball games are terrific but make sure you pay special attention to the little day-to-day communication. It's so much better to over communicate than under communicate, especially with a small team.

On Your Own? Get a Mentor, AKA Coach

An Olympic athlete is one of the most gifted or talented people in the world, but that have a coach. Even professional boxers, MMA fighters, fortune 500 CEO have a mentor or coach.

If you are a first time entrepreneur it is essential that you recruit a mentor to give advice, offer moral support, and break up the routine. A mentor is someone who can offer you wisdom, creativity, connections, accountability, credibility, and fresh thinking about your business. Meet with your mentor at least once a quarter to discuss your business and make certain that your mentor is willing to challenge you.

If your mentor has experience in your industry she/he can certainly provide you with specific in-the-trenches insight, but it is not necessary that a mentor have a similar background to you. In fact, it is often more valuable if a mentor has a different set of skills and background to bring that fresh perspective.

A mentor does not run your company, but has the expertise and wisdom to be there to help guide you through the many fit falls that are in being a business owner.

I've been in the entertainment industry for many years and I had a mentor. I could figure out why I was still not financially where I though I should be. One day my mentor gave me a life changing idea for the business and me. As mentioned earlier, I am an event planner and one of the biggest hurdles I had in that industry, is that you are only as good as your last event. Bootstrapping the startup I lacked the day-to-day funds to pay my personal bills and plan for the next event. I was making good money, but the problem was the cost of doing business and staying on top of the competition was costly.

My mentor one day asked me a question. What was my core passion and I told him music and he then help me to find the cash flow needed to sustain the business and me. He suggested that I open a record store. He explained that I have product knowledge, great customer, know my target market like no other and I already had inventory. Off I went and opened a store and it worked. It worked so well that I ended up opening up several locations.

On having a mentor gave me what I could see for myself. He coached me in how to start and run a business that I had no experience. But I had passion, drive and experience in the arena, I just need a outside person to help me to see other options.

A good mentor will sees what you may not and coach you into success!

Expanded Mentor Strategy:

As you grow your business, step up from a single individual to a multi-member advisory board. This will give you the opportunity to broaden even further the backgrounds and demographics of your advisors. Mentors and people you ask to be on your board will be honored to play that role and enjoy networking with each other too.

Mastermind Groups

Today, there what is called "mastermind groups." These group of people objective is to help each other to grow. They meet and the goal of the group is to listen, guide and support. Depending on the group is how in-depth they help each other.

The concept of the **Mastermind Group** was formally introduced by Napoleon Hill in the early 1900's. In his timeless classic, "Think And Grow Rich" he wrote about the **Mastermind** principle as: "The coordination of knowledge and effort of two or more people, who work toward a definite **purpose**, in the spirit of harmony."

7 Reasons To Join A Mastermind Group

How does a mastermind work? A group of smart people meet weekly, monthly, daily even if it makes sense, to tackle challenges and problems together. They lean on each other, give advice, share connections and do business with each other when appropriate. It's very much peer-to-peer mentoring and if you are lucky enough to get invited to one, you will most likely see a marked change in yourself and your business.

Here are 7 reasons why a mastermind might be right for you:

1. **You'll be part of an exclusive community.** Joining a mastermind typically involves you being invited by the members or going through an application process. The other members need you just as much as you need them, so quality of experience and knowledge is crucial to all involved.

2. **Advisement.** Once you are involved in a mastermind, that feeling of "being alone" while running your business is gone. The other members of the group turn into business advisors of sorts and vice versa.

3. **Collaboration is the name of the game.** You may find someone in the group that is a perfect fit to work on a project with you. Or, you may be the perfect person to help another member as well. The group works together collaboratively, to achieve more together.

4. **Extend your network.** Joining a mastermind expands your network exponentially and rapidly. If you are in business, you know how important your network is. By joining a mastermind, you instantly add to your network and typically gain the networks of those in the group with you.

5. **New learning.** Everyone in the mastermind is unique in skill, experience and connections. By interacting and sharing your challenges, it's almost certain that someone in your mastermind will have a solution for you and you may also be able to offer a solution, connection or tactic to help another in the group.

6. **Cross-promotion.** When you join a mastermind, you will most likely find ways to help each other by utilizing cross promotion. Finding ways to help each other through promoting to your respective networks.

7. **Think bigger.** Being in a mastermind will truly give you a Master Mind! You can't help but think bigger and stretch beyond your boundaries when surrounded by amazing people doing amazing things.

Masterminds are incredible and can do wonders for your business as well as for you, personally. Growing in a group is not only more effective, it's quite a bit more fun!

Establish a Brand

One of the most important assets you can develop for your business is a powerful brand. Brands are not just logos or tag lines. Brands are the culmination of who you are, how you're different from your competition, and why a buyer should do business with you.

Whether you're an established company or small start-up, a brand has tremendous impact. A brand instills confidence, creates loyalty, and many times can command a premium price. But most of all a great brand reduces a buyer's perception of risk and makes the purchase choice easy.

Developing a brand is much more than just deciding on a name or picking some colors. A brand is the sum of all you do. It's derived from all your touch points with your customers and prospects. Developing a brand requires having a plan that consistently communicates what your company is and does, along with your distinct attributes, image, and personality.

Branding consultant and author Karen Post, compares this notion to a "brain tattoo"—put there by choice, but which certainly can be removed at any time. That, by the way, is the name of her latest book, *Brain Tattoos, Creating Unique Brands that Stick to your Customers' Minds*. Her book delves into many creative ways companies and people can build and leverage their brand.

In this step we look at some of Karen Post's recommendations and action items for establishing a super brand:

1. Draft your brand DNA or essence
2. Define and relate to your target audience
3. Choose a brand name
4. Create a logo
5. Make a list of all your other touch points
6. Create a demand for your brand

Recommendations and action items

Draft your Brand DNA or Essence—Purpose, Points of Difference, Personality, and Promise

This is the foundation for everything you do and should guide your business, marketing, and communication decisions. These are your draft brand drivers. As you move through the following process, you may tweak those drivers or add something completely new. But at the end of the day, you should clearly define:

- **Your brand purpose:** a logical snapshot of what you provide the market.
- **Your brand points of difference:** things that are truly distinct that your competitors can't copy. While great customer service is important, it's not a point of difference; many of your competitors will claim the same thing. A point of difference can include a visual symbol, story, color scheme, proprietary process or product, historic milestone, physical characteristic, or combination of several of these.
- **Your brand personality:** a collection of human-like traits and adjectives that best describe your brand.
- **Your brand promise:** the emotional side of your purpose. If you were a tailor, your purpose would be to make and alter clothes and your promise would be to give people confidence when their clothing fits just right.

Define and Relate to your Target Audience

This means understanding your audience's age, sex, ethnicity, income, education level and locale. What motivates them to buy? How do they think? What are their hot buttons? Set up customer profiles, even if it's just in a simple spreadsheet. If you've done your homework and created your business plan, chances are you already have your target audience defined.

Choose a Brand Name

While your name is certainly not everything, it is an important piece to building a lasting brand.

Great brand names:

- Are emotional
- Stick on the brain
- Have personalities
- Have depth to tell stories and communicate with

As soon as you pick a name for your company, secure a domain name that is consistent with your brand name. You should also research trademark availability.

Should a name be literal and descriptive or obscure and emotional? There are strong arguments on both sides. Leaning toward the obscure and emotional can lead to very distinctive brands, which the literal and descriptive can speed up the process of communicating your message to your audience. Each case is unique and sometimes brand names get passed down and changing them would take an act of Congress.

Be original

Generic names like Computer Solutions, Performance Printing, or Innovative Technologies will just make you spend more and work harder at building a brand. They don't have legs and will likely drown in the sea of sameness. Being descriptive - as opposed to being generic - is not a bad thing for names. Given your limited budget, it can actually be a great way to go. Try to be original so your name stands out, so it means something, so you can own it, and so it will be much harder to copy.

Avoid names that are hard to spell or pronounce

BizHelp101.com provides inexpensive solutions to check for and reserve your business name.

- Name Check
- Name Reservation

Ask yourself, how will the market receive the name? With supporting context, will the market get it? Will it jive with your strategic positioning of the brand? Are there negative connotations or associations with the name?

Is there a magic, foolproof method for testing names?

No. In fact, sometimes too much analysis just delays decisions and defeats the whole mission of naming your brand before the next decade. I recommend that you test a little, listen a little to people you respect, listen to your gut feelings, and proceed with a choice.

While the brand name is very important, a brand cannot survive on name alone. The brand name and how the brand is executed are equally vital for a successful and sustained brand life. A great brand name can serve as the anchor to your cause, a symbol to your story, a point of difference in your marketplace, a memory trigger, or just one important part of your branding arsenal.

Tip & Warning This is a big one when choosing a name. One division of my company is helping new music artists to learn the business of making music and selling it. I called when I first launched it called "Musicpreneur." The meaning was good, it was cleaver, had the domain name for it, but there was a big unforeseen problem with the name. NO one could spell it. I have a good friend 30 years in the music industry tell me that most music recording artists can't even spell entrepreneur, so how are they going to spell Musicpreneur. Pryor to my friend telling me this, I was wondering why people weren't coming to the site. I was marketing, and promoting, mainly producing seminars and webinars, but next to no one signed up. The concept was not a failure, it was the name. I changed the name to iMusic Boss and over night it changes.

Please don't let your EGO keep you from chucking a name, it is only as good as someone can spell and find you!

Create a Logo

A logo is the visual image of your company that will be used in a variety of applications. When you are considering a design, think simple. Some of the best logos are one color and for a start-up, this can save you printing expenses.

Test how it photo copies and works in a digital environment. Sample other venues that you may grow into like an outdoor sign, moving vehicle, or promotional items like t-shirts and golf hats.

Make a List of all your Other Touch Points

Every time you touch a customer or prospect, you should feel your brand breathing. This can include your environment, other promotional activities, and even how your phone is answered. Remember the brand is the sum of you; infuse as many contact areas as possible with your brand essence or DNA.

Create a Demand for your Brand

Your product's performance, your customer service, follow-through, and your communication add up to a brand experience. Great experiences turn your brand into a magnet for new and repeat business. Buyers will seek you out, tell their friends, and remain loyal. Your brand can make the buyer's choice easy. **That is the power of the brand**.

Tip & Warning When developing you logo DO NOT make it so busy, meaning un-legible that prospective clients won't understand or able to read you name. When you look at fortune 500 companies and look at their logo, they are clean, short and bold. Being creative should be in your marketing, advertising you company. Your logo represents you and that will establish your first impression to prospective clients. Nike's logo is What? The name with the swoosh. As a matter of fact they did a whole campaign on using just the Swoosh and because it was simple distinctive, it works. Within Target's logo is a red target, they no longer use the word target they use a bulls-eye as their brand.

Again I'm going to use an old saying "Simpler is better," and when it comes to a logo that is a good policy. We tend to put our heart before logic, and that's a recipe for disaster. The goal must be within your logo an image that could be branded into greatness and not obscurity or an hot mess.

Market and Sell

This last step in our startup process is all about getting the word out about your business so customers come through your door (or perhaps to your homepage).

First and foremost, you'll need to study up on your target audience to develop a marketing message that will resonate with them.

Once you've got a grasp of how to best express the "special sauce" of what you offer, make sure you maintain that message consistently throughout your marketing efforts. It should be reinforced repeatedly to build on your brand identity and to give people a clear reason to be interested in your business.

To get you up the curve on marketing, we'll first give you an approach to defining your target market. That will get you prepared for setting a strategy to move forward. We'll provide an overview of the types of materials and a menu of marketing tactics to choose from – it's up to you to pick the methods that apply best to your opportunity.

We touch on three essential marketing items in this step:

1. Research & Strategy
2. Marketing Materials
3. Marketing Methods

Tip & Even though these are last they are the most important in building a successful business. You can have a life-changing, one of a kind idea and you don't know how to get it to the people who needs it, than those that will either need or want your product won't even know you exist.

Doing Market Research & Setting a Marketing Strategy

Just as you have to do intensive research for your business plan, you should also do a healthy amount of fact-finding in order to put together a well-oiled marketing strategy. If you do, your marketing effort will be much more methodical and effective.

The more time that you spend on who is your target market will more than likely save you in the long run. I have made BIG mistakes in not really looking into my target market. I have found that I'm not alone, I believe now that this I probably the most important aspect in pre-planning for your business.

To get started on your marketing strategy, answer the following questions:

Who is your typical buyer?

- What's a description of your target market? For example: "mothers, age 25-45, urban location, $90,000 household income, college-educated."

How do your potential customers' habits and behavior play into their purchasing decisions?

- What are their "hot buttons"?
    - Specific pain points, such as
        - Time delay
        - Shipping cost
        - Credit card security concerns
    - Urgent offers, such as "This offer ends tomorrow at midnight "
    - Getting a great deal
    - Being "first" to get it (people referred to as "early adopters")
    - Being trendy (must have the latest and hottest)
    - Hand-holding and personal attention (relationships rule their pocket book

How do you know they want what you offer?

- What related purchases do they make that give you confidence they'd be interested in what you offer?

How much are they willing to pay?

- You've got to figure out the all-important matter of pricing. What price tag is best for what you offer? It basically comes down to a combination of what you need to make in order to achieve workable profit margins, and what prices your customers are willing to bear. Oftentimes, it's a challenge to get these two numbers to match up. So, ask yourself:
  - What's the right price, based on your costs and your estimate of the maximum amount your customers are willing to pay?
  - What form of payment will customers want to use?
  - For wholesalers, what terms of payment will they be willing to accept?

Where (and how) will your customers want to buy your product or service?

- In-person or online? Via catalog or phone? From a trusted retail store?

How many people are in the overall market you're going after? And how many of them are reasonably strong candidates to be customers?

- The flaw in this logic is that it's extremely difficult to reach most of those people with a marketing message. How, practically, are you going to get through the rural rice paddies to let an average Chinese person know that you want to sell them something? And where are those people going to get the money to buy it in the first place?! Instead of using Chinese math, it's important to segment the total market down into sectors that have the highest likelihood of purchasing what you offer. And while the number might not start with a "b" like "billion," there still could be millions of very appealing people who are viable potential customers. It's crucial that you don't "buy into your own hype" as we like to warn. Get real with the answers to questions like this.

Why would your potential customers buy from you instead of your competition?

- This assumes your target market already demonstrates a desire to use or purchase something like what you offer. Is this so? If not, educating your customer will be critically important in your marketing. And that can be very expensive and time-consuming.
- You must know what your "value proposition" is – a crystal clear statement that anyone could understand but, most importantly, your targeted customer would quickly "get" about why they should be interested in what you offer.

What media has the greatest impact with your target market?

- Your choices are as varied today as they've ever been. There's everything from billboards at the roadside to animated online banners, from sandwich board-toting hucksters to direct mail through the mail slot, from online radio to cable TV, and from magazines to local classified ads. With this many options, or "noise," as we like to call it, coming at your prospective customer, it's more and more difficult to be sure your offering will stand out and get the attention you want it to. Just be sure you know to what they're tuned in to so you can be confident your marketing efforts will get noticed.

With all of these questions answered, it's time to start weaving a marketing strategy together.

The Right Marketing Materials

Once you have your target audience well defined, you're in a much better position to know what marketing materials would be appealing and useful to your audience.

There are basic printed materials you should consider - things like business cards, letterhead and brochures. These kinds of materials are essential for your communication, networking and sales activities.

One way to make the most of the dollars you spend is to create materials that have information that will stay true and accurate for the longest possible period of time. Things change often in a young business, so when possible use "evergreen," long-lasting information. Include inserts with the latest, greatest info that you print on your own.

Another key to developing good marketing materials without breaking the bank is to identify an affordable graphic designer and printer that will work with you. A local source for this can be a great help. Online sources are completely viable as well in this day and age of broadband internet access.

Marketing – a Menu of Methods

There are various types of marketing for you to consider. Below you'll find an overview of:

1. Grassroots Marketing
2. Public Relations
3. Affiliate Marketing
4. Online Marketing
5. Traditional Advertising

Grassroots Marketing

This is certainly the most affordable type of marketing. It consists of using resources you already have to spread the word about your product or service.

- Distribute your marketing materials (business cards, brochures, flyers) at local businesses, schools, churches and community centers.
- Give great customer service, and then ask customers to spread the word about your company and/or to write testimonials about their positive experience with your company.
- Participate in local/community events.
- Write an article and pitch it to local papers or niche publications.
- Word-of-mouth – tell friends, family and acquaintances and ask them to tell 5 people. Talk about your business every chance you get.
- Give out free samples of your product.

We give one form of grassroots marketing special attention – networking. Networking is a great, low cost way to connect with potential customers and strategic partners and spread the news about your business.

Chambers of commerce are great venues for this—they provide an ecosystem of members who are all looking for business, as well as sources of products and services.

Joining a chamber is extremely important to expanding your network, while at the same time, as a member you may be entitled to great discounts on services you might need, such as office supplies, telecommunications, health insurance, etc.

Resource

Chamber of Commerce
Find your local area chamber of commerce

Trade associations for your particular industry are another great networking resource you should consider. Oftentimes these associations hold events, offer industry-specific education and message boards online, and provide an opportunity for members to list their businesses on their website.

Resource

The ASAE Gateway to Associations Directory is a great resource for locating associations near you and is updated daily.

Public Relations

Use this example press release to help draft your own press releases.

Watch TV? Do much reading? Listen to talk radio? The news that you experience comes from a combination of reporters uncovering their own story themes and pitches sent to reporters by outside sources. As a new entrepreneur with a great business fresh on the scene, you may have a highly appealing story that reporters are interested in learning and writing about. And if they do write about your business, it can be a homerun opportunity for you.

We often refer to "the power of PR," a phenomenal way to generate awareness about what you're up to--virtually for free--that will touch potentially thousands or millions of people. Many entrepreneurs say their PR efforts have benefited them in ways they could never have afforded to pay for. Doesn't that sound tempting?

The question for you should be whether you choose to do your PR in-house or, instead, use a professional like Rembrandt Communications or BizHelp101.com. There are pros and cons to both strategies. As for doing it in-house:

Pros of in-house PR

- Your passion is contagious and gets the reporter's attention
- You control the message more closely

Cons of in-house PR

- You're an amateur and your pitch to reporters may seem that way
- You don't have the preexisting media contacts that a professional has

Affiliate Marketing

Affiliate marketing involves hooking up with other businesses or organizations that share a similar target audience to yours. With affiliate marketing, you work out a mutually beneficial relationship through which you swap advertising or share revenues with the other organization, and reach more people with your marketing message.

Resources

- LinkShare provides the technology to track, manage, and analyze the performance of sales, marketing, and business development initiatives.

- Commission Junction provides advanced performance-based marketing solutions that help marketers increase online leads and sales, by facilitating strategic relationships between advertisers and publishers.
- The Kolimbo Open Network offers programs for affiliates seeking additional revenue as well as merchants looking to promote their site across its network of affiliates.
- Biz Help 101 has a solution that through their affiliate marketing strategy has a team of Independent Consultants selling your products for you.

Online Marketing

These days a website is essential. And depending upon your niche and your objectives, it can be a major part of your marketing initiatives. Creating a website can be made fairly simple by working with a company that specializes in helping small businesses create their web presence.

But how about getting the word out about your site, and getting visitors to come back again and again? It's important to fill your website with content that's effective. It's what you say and how you say it that makes all the difference online. The content (words) on your site must be crisp and intelligent. What you say should grab a visitor's attention, establish credibility, pique their interest and motivate them to action.

There are a number of ways to promote your business online, here's just a sample of the most popular methods:

- **Online display advertising** – the "granddaddy" of online advertising, involving the purchase of display space on a popular website. Everyone has seen 'banner' ads at the top of websites – despite reports of their demise, display ads are still popular for their reach and for the branding effectiveness of graphical ads.
- **Search engine marketing** – this catch-all has two primary marketing tools under its umbrella; search engine advertising and search engine optimization. Both involve driving traffic from the hundreds of millions of eyeballs that scan search results on Google, Yahoo, MSN and other search engines, but the approach is drastically different – be sure you understand the distinctions.
- **Email marketing** – along with online display ads, email marketing got a bad rap, mostly thanks to spammers clogging your inbox with offers to refinance your mortgage. But with new rules and regulations, and much stricter controls on spam, getting your message out through email is enjoying a revival. Email can be an outstanding customer retention tool, so you'll want it to be part of your online marketing mix.

Resources

- Biz Help 101 offers a powerful Internet Marketing Suite that will help you to effective market your business.
- For help on Search Engine Advertising, check out Yahoo's Search Marketing, or Google AdWords.

Traditional Advertising

Traditional paid advertising includes the things so many of us are already familiar with (and encounter so often in everyday life). Think of things like billboards, magazine and newspaper ads, broadcast spots such as those on TV and radio, and even direct mail pieces that seem to clog your mailbox each day.

In the previous section we discussed online display advertising, which is often paid for on a "cost-per-thousand" impressions ("CPM") basis. In other words, the people selling you the advertising space price their opportunity based on the specific reach of that advertising. The same pricing model applies to traditional advertising methods, where the reach of the advertising medium – whether it's the size of a subscription list, listenership, or viewership – will determine the rate you'll pay to reach that audience.

Advertising can do the following:

- Attract new customers, prospects and leads
- Encourage existing customers to spend more on your product or service
- Build credibility, establish and maintain your "brand" or unique business identity, and enhance your reputation
- Inform or remind customers and prospects of the benefits your business has to offer
- Promote your business to customers, investors or others and slowly build sales

Should your business warrant advertising (and your pocketbook allow for it), it's important to create an advertising plan and budget in advance.

Points to consider:

- Who is in your target market and what mediums are grabbing their attention?
- When obtaining rate card information, be sure to understand how many of your ad impressions are reaching your target audience vs. those who are not in your target audience. And ALWAYS negotiate published rates.
- "Frequency! Frequency! Frequency!" Is the name of the game. That's why it's important to create a comprehensive six-month or year-long plan

before you even take out your first ad, so you know you can afford to advertise on a frequent basis. Signing up for a frequency rate will allow you to spend less per ad, if you do this from the beginning.

- If you are advertising in print publications, always ask your sales rep for the best positioning. A right-hand page, for example, may get many more viewings than a left-hand page.
- Create advertisements that generate a response you can measure. Examples include coupons, which are redeemed in stores or include a specific web address that customers visit for redemption.
- Make sure your advertisements stay true to your brand and are consistent with all other marketing mediums.

I wrote another guide called Startup Guide to Marketing that goes into more details on advertising, marketing, promotions, branding. You can find it at www.StartupGuideto.com.

Conclusion

The Startup Guide to Be Your Own Boss hopefully has empowered you to start and get your business up and running. Make sure you go through and write a business plan and work the plan. Being a business owner will be hard work, but the reward is that you will do what you love.

Adapt

If a plan doesn't work adapt and change it. A plan is just a guide and not an absolute. Keep in mind that everything you implement will work and you need to know when to as the old country singer sang "to know then to fold them and know when to walk away."

Adapt to your surrounding and trends. Your community may and will change and you will need to adapt to stay relevant. Many businesses that I have consulted were not willing to change with the times and their business died.

Tip & Warning If you remember that I wrote about having music stores. Then I sold records, cassette tapes, Cd's and my mentor one day told me to read a music business trade publication called Billboard magazine, that there was an article that I needed to read. That article was about a new startup online company called Napster. The article told me that traditional music stores were going to die and if I tried to stay in a brick and mortar store and not embraced the change that was coming it would destroy me and my income and the business. 99% of traditional record stores had to close their door and I got out because I was not married to the store, I'm an entrepreneur and we adapt. There is a movie called Bebe's Kids and the kids throughout the whole movie would say "we don't die we multiply" and that is us, the entrepreneur, we don't die we adapt!

Tell Somebody

Once you have started your business, join a business network and tell everyone that you have started your business. The business network will keep you encouraged and you should get some business. We offer a support system that if you have any questions or you get stuck our professional team of consultants is either a fingertip or a phone call away. For more details go to http://www.BizHelp101.com or call me at 1-657-204-6249. God Bless and get going today!